What Ot

"I just finished reading your book at 3:00 a.m.! I then spent an additional hour in prayer. I have to admit that I've been blessed to find myself in an atmosphere of prayer for the last several decades being mentored and surrounded by the likes of Pastor Cymbala. Having said that, your book was like a *kairos* moment for me personally. It's dangerous to get 'used to' the atmosphere of prayer. I have been GREATLY encouraged and freshly motivated to pursue God THROUGH PRAYER in response to the cry of your heart in *Inevitable & Imminent*."

—CHARLES HAMMOND, PH.D.
ASSOCIATE DEAN OF STUDENT LIFE, NYACK COLLEGE
ASSOCIATE MINISTER, BROOKLYN TABERNACLE CHURCH

"As a former business director for several years at a national telecommunications service provider and now pastor and university professor, I know the usefulness of a coherent process. *Inevitable and Imminent: On Becoming a House of Prayer—The Process*, is the well thought-out and real-world blueprint to help churches move towards that significant spiritual goal of becoming a house of prayer. Dr. Carrington outlines an authentic process that will stimulate any spiritual leader who is truly seeking to grow their congregation. Amazingly, the growth potential associated with this process has more to do with spiritual growth and not merely membership and/or financial growth. As a result of reading this book, I'm now persuaded and encouraged to underscore these biblical principles in my church. This book is powerful and on point!"

—HUGH MARRIOTT, D.MIN.
PASTOR, ALLEN TEMPLE AME CHURCH
ADJUNCT PROFESSOR, LONG ISLAND UNIVERSITY

"*Inevitable and Imminent* will only change your life if you read it and then adhere to the message within. Please take the time to read it, folks. This book is a wonderful blessing."

—DAVID JOHANNESSEN

"*Inevitable and Imminent* emphasizes the primary importance of prayer in the body of Christ, the church. Dr. Carrington pulls together biblical information and his own personal prayer journey to challenge the readers of this volume to take God's people higher. This book is not another book about prayer through some sort of mechanistic process; rather, this book underscores the essence of spending quality time in corporate prayer in our churches. Dr. Carrington highlights the irony of the situation in his assessment of the prayerlessness that exists in many churches when churches are called upon to become 'houses of prayer.' This book is a must-read because it is biblical, radical, practical, personal, forthright, and thought-provoking. I would recommend this volume to every person who is associated with a church, and more specifically, every person in church leadership. *Inevitable and Imminent* was a great read, and I have no doubt that you will enjoy your journey with this book."

—**MARLON ROBINSON**
PASTOR
CEO AND CO-FOUNDER OF FAMILY ON POINT

"It has been a deep spiritual experience reading through this valuable document, Hugh. The Lord has given you something special, and you are wise enough to do something about it! In this book, I particularly like how you stated your presuppositions at the beginning and how the diagrams used expand and become clearer as the chapters progress. Your personal experiences and the journey you invite us to share with you add validity and credibility to this book. You have a meaningful, informative, practical, and spiritual approach. I love it!"

—**DION T. HARRIGAN, PH.D.**
PASTOR, BETHANY SDA CHURCH
PROFESSOR OF EDUCATION, NYACK COLLEGE

"The Old Testament scholar and founder of the Biblical Seminary in New York, Wilbert Webster White, famously said, 'Prayer works, prayer is work, prayer leads to work.' Dr. Carrington's book takes the genius of White's profound statement and breaks it into understandable and digestible parts informed by the latest insights from the sociological and business worlds and the eternal truths of scripture. If your evangelical church is stuck in neutral, Dr. Carrington's insight and guidance may just be what you need to get moving again."

—THE REV WILLIAM WEISENBACH, DMIN, DD
RETIRED PRESBYTERIAN MINISTER
FORMER ACADEMIC VICE PRESIDENT
OF NEW YORK THEOLOGICAL SEMINARY

"I purchased this book and met Hugh at the Northern Adirondack Camp Meeting last summer. This book is a sure thing of a blueprint to get churches on the road to innovative ways of growth. Families can follow the advice in this book to heal and grow into more loving family units. It's just an all-around self-help healing book that leads one to Jesus. The emphasis is simple: 'PRAYER!' Who would have ever 'thunk' it? Something as simple as prayer. We have to start somewhere, and this book will get churches of all sizes on the right track to spiritual growth! I highly recommend it, and anyway possible, do go see Hugh in person and listen to his message! And do so prayerfully. Brother Hugh, I'm still relishing in the lessons you shared with us this past weekend! I plan to encourage my church family to initiate some of your lessons in this book—our new road map to better church growth!"

—DORA MOSE

"On last Wednesday, I led out at prayer meeting. My three-to-five minute 'word' regarding Spiritual Robbers was well-received. One of the members commented, 'Man, you are wading in some deep waters...' Hugh, I think that was a compliment (LOL)! Regarding the takeaways and summarizations captured from your book... For me, you're running with E. M. Bounds and Cymbala. I know, I know...that's God...and I praise Him. I am being richly blessed by it."

—DEXTER RAVENELL

"Transformation is not an event, but rather a progressive process that leads to glory. Proverbs 4:18 tells us, '...the path of the just is like the shining sun, that shines ever brighter unto the perfect day.' Hugh makes practical the process of this progressive journey of kingdom glory in *Inevitable & Imminent: On Becoming a House of Prayer—The Process.* When these gems are understood and applied in our personal lives and ministries, the results will cause us to utter the words of Peter, '...we have the prophetic word confirmed, which you do well to heed as a light that shines in a dark place, until the day dawns and the morning star rises in your hearts...' (II Peter 1:19, NKJV).

—PASTOR ROHAN SPENCER
YOUTH DEVELOPMENT COUNSELOR & ASSOCIATE MINISTER
HANSON PLACE SEVENTH-DAY ADVENTIST CHURCH

"In *Inevitable and Imminent*, Dr. Carrington provides profound insight to the question: what is the quality of your individual and corporate prayer life? Prayerfulness is the hallmark of spiritual potency, and prayerlessness reflects spiritual impotency. Whenever churches regulate prayer to a secondary or tertiary position, those institutions quickly approach the precipice of spiritual irrelevancy."

—ROLAND H. ROBINSON
ASSISTANT DEAN STUDENT AFFAIRS, LIU BROOKLYN
ASSOCIATE MINISTER, BROWN MEMORIAL BAPTIST CHURCH

"Dr. Hugh Carrington's volume is a must-read keepsake for church leaders at all levels. This very insightful and robust analysis of the spiritual malaise characterizing many of our churches today and the simple, practical, tested and proven prescriptions offered to revitalize and energize congregations make the volume extremely useful—not only for church leaders, but also to individual members. Those who read and apply the wisdom of these pages will experience revival in their own lives and see God unleash His power in their church."

—JEREMIAH COX, SR.
FIRST ELDER, HANSON PLACE SDA CHURCH

"I have long held the belief that the Word of God—the Bible—is a book of patterns and principles upon which one can build a successful church, business, marriage, life, etc. Dr. Hugh Carrington's book, *Inevitable & Imminent: On Becoming a House of Prayer—The Process*, confirms my belief. Dr. Carrington adeptly mines the Word of God and illustrates the blueprint and principles that will transform any ministry or individual.

Inevitable & Imminent boldly demonstrates with clarity that power to transform flows from proclaiming the Word of God and lays out the simple, yet profound, process of becoming 'a house of prayer for all peoples,' which in turn will transform a life, a family, a ministry, a community, a city, or a nation. *Inevitable & Imminent* is a must-read for anyone who wishes to become a transformational leader of this generation and revive and fulfil Christ's directive for His church—becoming 'a house of prayer for all peoples.' Catch the vision; receive the power."

—T. S. WEEKS
MINISTRY LEADER

"Okay, wow! Overall a bold, yet enlightening read! I kept shaking my head, asking why then are we in church if not for prayer? I feel like the blinders have been removed. I had no idea prayer has become secondary to everything else. In true form, you did an excellent job addressing the risks of straying from/diminishing prayer, and outlining ways to self-correct. You inspire me."

—EVVA ASSING-MURRAY, PH.D.
PUBLIC HEALTH ANALYST, HEALTH AND HUMAN SERVICES
ADJUNCT LECTURER, MONTGOMERY COLLEGE

Inevitable
& Imminent

On Becoming a House of Prayer
– The Process

Bridge Press

This book is dedicated to all houses of prayer.

Spiritual matters are spiritually discerned—
before you begin and while you're reading,
pray for spiritual discernment.

Contents

Acknowledgments   i

Preface   iii

Introduction   xi

Chapter 1   The Vision   1

Chapter 2   Spiritual Robbers   19

Chapter 3   The Proclamation   35

Chapter 4   Fruitful Ministries   51

Chapter 5   Attacks and Distractions   69

Chapter 6   Walk Away Praying   79

Chapter 7   Try Again   89

Chapter 8   A Formative Summary   103

Chapter 9   The Pronouncement   115

Conclusion   133

My Prayer   159

House of Prayer Indicator Assessment   161

A Guide to Reading and Praying Through
Inevitable & Imminent in 40 Days   173

Notes to the Reader   201

About the Author   205

Acknowledgments

I would like to begin by thanking my wife (angel, investor, attorney and manager) and daughter for their holistic investment to ensure the success of this project and all future projects. In addition, I must thank so many others (family and friends) for their assistance. The supportive individuals are too many to list, so I will not catalog names for fear of leaving out someone. I've said thank you privately, and now I want to say it again—thank you!

Preface

The Holy Spirit began a process with me in late-summer 2004. However, not until after ending a prayer session with my prayer partner on November 17, 2005, was the concept for this volume fully revealed to me. It was early afternoon, and the workday was not over; yet I was unable to continue with my employer's work. I spent the rest of that afternoon and evening in the quiet of my office, listening to the Holy Spirit and taking notes. He spoke clearly, and He was very specific. I was obedient, and He kept sharing. By Saturday evening, November 19, 2005, the concept was fully outlined on paper (see Figure 1).

A few weeks later while traveling to New York City, I received a call asking me to speak for Sabbath worship at my local church. I hesitated to accept the invitation because I feared I would not have enough time to prepare a sermon. I was planning a trip for the upcoming Christmas holiday, and I was also in the process of relocating to New York City. Moreover, my intent was not to return to the pulpit at that church. I had planned to attend as usual, take my regular seat, and quietly walk away, praying to New York City.

With the encouragement of the Holy Spirit, I embraced the challenge and accepted the invitation. I developed an outline for the sermon (which became the prototype for this volume) and preached what turned out to be my farewell sermon on January 28, 2006. The sermon was titled "It's Inevitable." I thought the Holy Spirit had shared all with me concerning the process back in November, but to my surprise, there was more. As I ended the sermon that afternoon, the Holy Spirit revealed bold new thoughts about His pronouncement on churches that disregard His command to be houses of prayer.

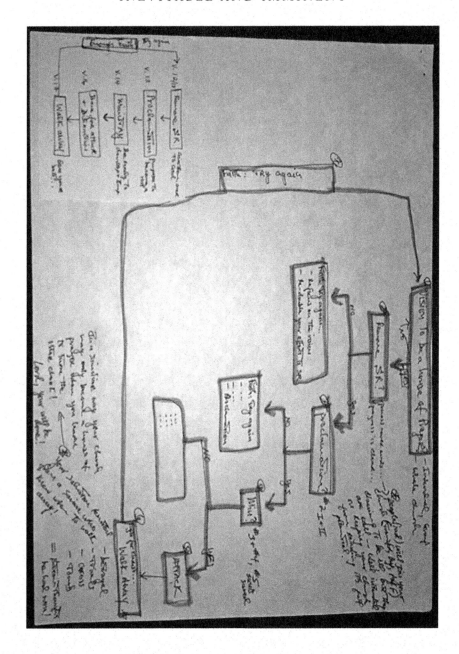

Figure 1. First Draft of "The Process"

The concept was clear in my mind, and the outline was on paper. During the sermon, I was able to articulate the process whereby a church would become a house of prayer; both God and the congregation were pleased. Moreover, God had allowed me to experience, firsthand, the entire process; I embodied and cast the vision on January 15, 2005, and walked away praying on January 28, 2006. Nevertheless, I procrastinated in my writing because everybody and anybody were writing about prayer, and I did not want to write *yet* another book on, about, or how to pray. It had to be more. "When prayer becomes this popular, we should begin to be on our guard."[1] Thus, I was hesitant, and I used this hesitancy as an excuse not to move forward.

I PROCRASTINATED IN MY WRITING BECAUSE I DID NOT WANT TO WRITE *YET* ANOTHER BOOK ON, ABOUT, OR HOW TO PRAY.

In his book, *If My People Pray*, Randy Maxwell states, "Lack of teaching on prayer isn't the problem—lack of implementation is."[2] In other words, we know all we need to know about prayer. Now we have to do it. As such, I struggled to make time to articulate what the Holy Spirit had shared with me. It was not until September 6, 2006, that I was impressed (or finally listened, if I'm to be totally honest) to refocus, and I began to write in earnest. I was again distracted by life in the spring of 2007. Then one Sabbath evening in December 2007, I heard His voice again and continued writing. Though I became distracted again, I never lost sight of what I needed to complete.

I find it amazing what God will do to get us to do what we know we have to do. In March 2014, my brother texted and suggested that we fast and pray as a family on Wednesdays. He also suggested that we read *The Circle Maker*. If you're talking prayer, I'm in—where do I sign up?

Charged by his suggestion, I downloaded the book and started reading. A few weeks later and several pages into chapter 7, everything changed when I came across the following statement:

"Too many authors worry about whether or not their book will get published. That isn't the question. The question is this: Are you called to write? That's the only question you need to answer. And if the answer is yes, then you need to write the book as an act of obedience. It doesn't matter whether anyone reads it or not."

—MARK BATTERSON[3]

I thought I was being obedient and compliant. After all, I had outlined the concept, preached the sermon, and had started writing the book. That act of obedience was not enough; I needed to finish. After reading that statement, I closed my eyes, bowed my head and silently acknowledged to God, "I hear You." As an act of obedience, I knew that I needed to write.

May 2015: I'm currently writing again, and I'm in the process of asking God to give me enough faith and the place to try it again.

I believe by the time you're finished reading this book, you'll be vexed—displeased—with yourself, God, or me. You'll be so displeased with yourself that you'll make the necessary changes. You'll be displeased with me because you've been convinced that you need to make some radical and difficult changes. Or you'll be displeased with God because you're now resisting the changes that you clearly know need to be made. My prayer is that you'll be displeased with yourself—not me or God—and make the fundamental changes.

BY THE TIME YOU'RE FINISHED READING THIS BOOK,
YOU'LL BE VEXED—DISPLEASED—
WITH YOURSELF, GOD, OR ME.

When I preached what turned out to be my farewell sermon on the morning of January 28, 2006, this was my prayer, and it continues to be my prayer as I write the following:

Father, my prayer today is for spiritual discernment. I pray that You will give us a clear vision of what You would have us to know. And then Lord, I pray that You would give me boldness to present Your word as it should be presented today.

Reflections

_____

_____

_____

_____

_____

_____

_____

_____

_____

_____

_____

_____

_____

_____

Notes

1 Richard W. O'Fill, *Transforming Prayer: Praying to Become Rather Than to Receive* (Hagerstown, Md.: Review and Herald Publishing Association, 1999), p. 109.

2 Randy Maxwell, *If My People Pray: An Eleventh-Hour Call to Prayer and Revival* (Nampa, Ida.: Pacific Press Publishing Association, 1995), p. 90.

3 Mark Batterson, *The Circle Maker: Praying Circles Around Your Biggest Dreams and Greatest Fears* (Grand Rapids: Zondervan, 2011), p. 101.

Introduction

I would like to begin by putting forth three presuppositions supported with biblical evidence with reference to the steadfastness and credibility of God, the obligatory status that prayer should have within the church, and the un-substitutable importance of prayer in finishing God's work.

- Presupposition #1: God does not change and cannot lie.
- Presupposition #2: Prayer is obligatory within the church.
- Presupposition #3: Prayer moves the hand of God.

God Does Not Change and Cannot Lie

"Think not that I am come to destroy the law, or the prophets: I am not come to destroy, but to fulfill. For verily I say unto you, Till heaven and earth pass, one jot or one tittle shall in no wise pass from the law, till all be fulfilled" (Matthew 5:17, 18, KJV). God does not change, and He cannot lie. If God were to change "one jot or one tittle," then the character of God would be questioned. And if the character of God were in doubt, then the law would be open to debate and change. *Stick with me; I'm going somewhere.*

"Every good gift and every perfect gift is from above, and cometh down from the Father of lights, with whom is no variableness, neither shadow of turning" (James 1:17, KJV). Again, God does not change. There is no variableness, meaning there is no irregularity in God—He is settled and predictable. In other words, "Jesus Christ the same yesterday, and to day, and for ever" (Hebrews 13:8, KJV).

If you still don't believe me, look at Malachi 3:6 (KJV), which states, "For I am the LORD, I change not; therefore ye sons of Jacob are not consumed." Finally, Numbers 23:19 (NKJV) states, "God is not a man, that He should lie, nor a son of man, that He should repent. Has He said, and will He not do? Or has He spoken, and will He not make it good?" Unlike many of us, God's Word is good.

Accordingly, we can conclude that God cannot change and does not lie. Therefore, when He made the statement "my house shall be called a house of prayer," what He meant was that our churches shall, they will, become houses of prayer. God's steadfastness and credibility guaranteed that this would happen.

The Obligatory Nature of Prayer

As Christians, we believe that "All scripture is given by inspiration of God, and is profitable for doctrine, for reproof, for correction, for instruction in righteousness" (2 Timothy 3:16, KJV). Whether found in the Old or New Testament, scripture must be taken seriously, honoring God through our obedience while holding Him to His Word.

The word *shall* is found throughout the Bible—calling us to action ("you shall" or "will do…") and telling of things to come ("…shall" or "will happen"). Look at the following examples:

- Genesis 2:24 (KJV)— "Therefore *shall* a man leave his father and his mother, and *shall* cleave unto his wife: and they *shall* be one flesh."

- Deuteronomy 6:17 (KJV)— "Ye *shall* diligently keep the commandments of the LORD your God, and his testimonies, and his statutes, which he hath commanded thee."

- Joshua 6:3 (KJV)— "And ye *shall* compass the city, all ye men of war, and go round about the city once. Thus *shalt* thou do six days."

- Malachi 3:10 (KJV)— "Bring ye all the tithes into the storehouse, that there may be meat in mine house, and prove me now herewith, saith the LORD of hosts, if I will not open you the windows of heaven, and pour you out a blessing, that there *shall* not be room enough to receive it."

- Matthew 1:21 (KJV)— "And she *shall* bring forth a son, and thou *shalt* call his name JESUS: for he *shall* save his people from their sins."

- Hebrews 10:37 (KJV)— "For yet a little while, and he that *shall* come will come, and will not tarry."

- Revelation 22:5 (KJV)— "And there *shall* be no night there; and they need no candle, neither light of the sun; for the Lord God giveth them light: and they *shall* reign for ever and ever."

Furthermore, Bible-believing Christians take the Word of God literally. As such, these Bible-believing Christians are quick to question the sexual orientation or the marriage-ability of any man or woman who appears to be avoiding or delaying leaving and cleaving. Recently, individuals have seen how insolence and high regard as to the keeping and status of the Ten Commandments has resulted in many court cases. On any given day, believers can be found extolling the faith of Joshua for marching on day seven when nothing had happened on day six. Many churches will question a person's loyalty and begin to debate the value of his membership for not returning the tithe. Therefore, Christians honor God and oblige the church, expecting that God will bless them.

That same expecting spirit allows us to faithfully celebrate the birth of Christ each year as we daily cling to the assurance of His forgiveness. Wrapped up in His birth and subsequent cleansing, through His death and resurrection, is the guarantee of salvation at His second coming, which we eagerly await. And when He does return, we anticipate spending days with Him that will never end, as we will reign with Him forever and ever. Still, the edict "my house shall be called a house of prayer," found in the same Bible is somehow altogether dismissed or grossly neglected.

How is the "shall" found in Matthew 21:13 any different? It is not. Like so many other verses, this verse also calls believers to action. To suggest that the Ten Commandments or tithing is any weightier scripturally or spiritually than making God's house (your church) a house of prayer is to question the intelligence and authority of God. Nevertheless, somehow prayer got classified as lesser-than. Yet prayer is also a scriptural edict, which is pregnant with promise—ask (pray) and it *shall* be given you (Matthew 7:7). Moreover, it is the only edict in scripture that permits us to have a direct and intimate relationship with God Himself.

As a result, a conclusion that the word "shall," as used in Matthew 21:13, is of no less importance than in other scriptural uses can be drawn. Therefore, when Jesus made the statement "my house shall be called a house of prayer," the obligatory and perpetual status that prayer should have within the church was clearly set down.

Prayer Moves the Hand of God

The Bible is bursting with example after example of how God moved when His people prayed. For instance:

- Abraham's prayer that God would save Sodom and Gomorrah and not destroy the righteous with the wicked (Genesis 18)

- Moses' prayer challenging God to protect His character and reputation and to honor His promises while showing mercy to Israel (Numbers 14)

- Joshua's prayer for more daylight, causing God to alter the course of nature—the sun and the moon stood still (Joshua 10)

- Hannah's prayer that God would remember her and bless her with a son (I Samuel 1)

- Asa's prayer to God for help as an army of one million men and three hundred chariots marched against him (II Chronicles 14)

- Nehemiah's prayer for God to strengthen his hands as he faced the seemingly insurmountable task of finishing the rebuilding of the wall (Nehemiah 6)

- The Gentile woman's prayer for her daughter who was grievously vexed with a devil (Matthew 15)

- The widow's unrelenting and determined prayer for justice (Luke 18)
- The apostles' prayer for the outpouring of the Holy Spirit (Acts 1)
- The promise of our answered prayers for mercy and favor at the throne of grace (Hebrews 4)

Of the many powerful prayers in the Bible, I want to focus on Abraham's prayer for Sodom and Gomorrah. During these last days, this prayer is an excellent illustration of how intercessory prayer (or the lack thereof) will be tied to souls being saved or lost—heaven and hell—before God destroys this earth. Furthermore, it will do us well to remember that many of the vices that caused Sodom and Gomorrah to be weighed and found wanting (Daniel 5:27), are many of, if not, the same vices that will produce a similar verdict for planet Earth in the not-too-distance future. But the question remains: what would happen if we prayed like Abraham?

Abraham boldly stood before God and prayed that He would save Sodom and Gomorrah if fifty righteous could be found within the city, and God responded. When you're praying and God is responding, it gives you added boldness to keep pressing Him in prayer. And so, Abraham did… "What if You found forty-five?" God responded. Realizing that if he continued to pray God would continue to respond, Abraham prayed… "What if You found 40…30…20…10? Each time he prayed, God responded; if we don't pray, God will not move.

Genesis 18:33 states, "And the LORD went His way…" The Lord excused Himself only after Abraham stopped praying. Abraham prayerfully negotiated his way from fifty down to ten righteous individuals and stopped. When he stopped praying, God stopped moving. Had he continued to pray, could the entire city of Sodom and Gomorrah have been saved? I can only assume that if God was willing to save the city for ten righteous individuals, He would have been equally as willing to do the same for nine or less.

Scripture is silent as to why Abraham stopped imploring God to save Sodom and Gomorrah. I'm not concerned, however, that he stopped praying, I'm more so encouraged by the fact that he had enough faith to keep praying for as long as he did. If we don't pray, God can't hear and will not be able to move on our behalf. So while we don't know why Abraham stopped praying, what we do know is that when he prayed, God heard and responded.

IN THESE LAST DAYS,

MORE THAN ANYTHING ELSE, GOD DESIRES

TO PARTNER WITH A PRAYING CHURCH.

Thus, we can conclude that if we don't pray, God will not move; prayer moves the hand of God. Therefore, when He made the statement, "my house shall be called a house of prayer," the un-substitutable importance of prayer as a means of finishing His work was charted. In these last days, more than anything else, God desires to partner with a praying church.

Inevitable and Imminent

Note that the word *shall* is an auxiliary verb, meaning that something is disposed to happen; it is capable of happening; it is expected to happen. When we use the word *shall*, future time is indicated and determination is expressed; it will happen. Another word gains significance when considering the future tense and determination wrapped up in the statement "my house shall be called a house of prayer."

That word is *inevitable*. Inevitable is an adjective, meaning that something is unable to be evaded or prevented. In other words, it is impossible to change it. When Jesus said, "my house shall be called a house of prayer," He meant that it was inevitable. It's expected, fated, inescapable, sure, anticipated, foreseeable, necessary, destined, irresistible, certain, unalterable, predictable, unavoidable, and I like this one—it is ordained.

As we consider the inevitability of the statement, "my house shall be called a house of prayer," we would do well to also consider the fact that it must happen soon. In other words, its fulfillment is imminent. *Imminent* means that "it's coming up, at hand, pending, forthcoming, on the agenda, on the horizon, just around the corner, looming...." God's house (the church) is going to become a house of prayer. It's about to happen. "Why?" you ask. Because last-day events demand a praying church.

So if we've reasoned correctly that:

1. God cannot change and does not lie,

2. Prayer is obligatory within the church, and

3. Prayer moves the hand of God,

then that means that His house (the church) will soon become a house of prayer. It will happen, and it will happen very soon; it's inevitable, and it's imminent.

If it is inevitable and imminent, then there must be a process whereby His house (our church) becomes a house of prayer. The process will be experienced at a micro (personal) level and at a macro (church) level. At the outset, you'll be personally impressed to make changes that will meaningfully impact your church. Your church (leaders and/or other members), in turn, will make adjustments that will either foster or impede the process of becoming a house of prayer.

Another Chance

The process of transitioning from church to house of prayer begins with the vision. After you've cast the vision that God's house must become a house of prayer, you have to begin the process of *prayerfully* removing spiritual robbers from His house. Next, you must proclaim your church to be a house of prayer. With this declaration, you'll immediately embark on the task of developing and implementing fruitful ministries. Know, however, that you will face attacks and distractions along the way. Consequently, you may have to walk away. Even so walk away praying, knowing that you must have enough faith to try again.

It is one thing for God to reveal Himself; however, it is an even greater spiritual privilege when He allows you to also experience what He has shared with you. God revealed this process to me, and then He decided, in His abundant wisdom, to allow me to experience the entire process, first-hand. Very few individuals would volunteer for an assignment that would take him/her to some of the greatest heights and then to some of the lowest, perceived lows. And neither did I. There I was, a broken and empty vessel trying to keep a low profile, but God was willing to take yet another chance to use me.

I quickly discovered that it was not about me, but about what I had and what He wanted to use. God had blessed me with the professional skills and education to help organizations develop, implement, and evaluate a variety of programs to achieve their goals. Now He wanted to use me to help churches understand, develop, and implement this process. He shared it with me, He allowed me to live it, and now I have to share it with you. Get ready to be blessed. If you're obedient to what you read, your life will never be the same.

IF YOU'RE OBEDIENT TO WHAT YOU READ,
YOUR LIFE WILL NEVER BE THE SAME.

Disruptive Theology

Because of the use of the adjective "disruptive," many perceive the term, *disruptive technology*, to be a negative expression. However, for most involved, the expression is very positive. A *disruptive technology* is "one that displaces an established technology and shakes up the industry." A completely new industry is created by this groundbreaking product. Recent examples of disruptive technologies include e-mail, USB flash drives, digital cameras, iTunes, and cloud computing—just to name a few.

These innovations changed traditional business methods and practices and drastically changed our way of life. As I have already noted, the majority of society welcomes disruptive technology because it has the potential to greatly enhance our lives. Where would we be today if digital cameras had not been developed? The segments of our society that consistently lament the arrival of new (disruptive) technology are the owners and producers of the old technology. Businesses that fail to continue growing and developing often find themselves displaced by the new technology. Consequently, their value added to, and their value in the marketplace, are greatly impacted.

When we consider disruptive technologies and their impact on firms, they fall into one of three groups. The firms that are able to create the new technology can become very profitable. Other firms adapt and are able to survive. Still, other firms are obliterated and become obsolete.[1] In the final analysis, the winner is the firm that introduced the new technology that offers a better and more effective way to do everything. These firms rewrite the rules in the marketplace. Accordingly, they're disruptive to business as usual.

Like disruptive technology, I pray that this volume will be a disruptive theology. I pray that this reminder of the importance of prayer will displace our established ways of thinking about prayer and shake up our churches—leaders and members, alike. I pray that the owners and producers of the old way of thinking about prayer will not lament the change. I pray that it will drastically change our way of life. I pray that our churches will add value in the spiritual marketplace. Finally, I pray that this volume will be disruptive to business as usually when it comes to prayer and that churches will not be obliterated and become obsolete, but that individuals and churches will adapt and survive. The process of becoming a house of prayer begins with the vision.

Reflections

_____

_____

_____

_____

_____

_____

_____

_____

_____

_____

_____

_____

_____

_____

Notes

[1]   Kenneth Laudon and Jane Laudon, *Management Information Systems: Managing the Digital Firm* (12th ed.; Upper Saddle River, N. J.: Prentice Hall, 2012), p. 87.

ONE

The Vision

*And said unto them, It is written,
My house shall be called the house of prayer....*

—MATTHEW 21:13 (KJV)

As I continued my studies on prayer, the Lord took me repeatedly to Matthew 21, emphasizing the process whereby a church becomes a house of prayer. The *first* phase (see Figure 2) in becoming a house of prayer is that of embodying the vision. At some point, you'll come to a profound understanding of the importance of prayer and of the significance it must have in God's house (your church). You will have some experience that will drive you to your knees. God is trying to get your attention. It may be a problem or it may be His favor, but He is trying to get your attention. The experience will drive you to your knees and buttress the value of prayer.

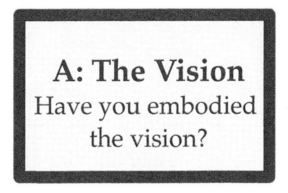

Figure 2. The Vision

The Rough Side of the Mountain

Unfortunately, for too many of us, the only way God can get our attention is through a crisis. God, in His wisdom, will take us up the rough side of the mountain. If He were to take most of us up the smooth side, we would slip right back into a state of ease, indolence, and halfhearted worship. "When times are smooth, our pursuit of God loses its edge of diligence, and often we're not even aware that it's happening."[1] We tell ourselves that we are rich and increased with goods and have need of nothing (Revelation 3:17). So God, in His astuteness, allows some trouble in our lives to make the way rough. This time of trouble allows us to hold on and to seek His face; we're driven to our knees.

Most of us don't recognize a crisis as an accelerator to the position to which we were heading in the first place. Jonah's physical and spiritual itinerary included Nineveh. Yes, it is true that the prophet was on his way to Tarshish (Jonah 1:3), but it was not where God had sent him. A crisis (the storm) accelerated him to go to the place where God had ordained him to be in the first place. Absent the crisis, it would have taken Jonah much longer to get to Nineveh.

Similarly, some of us are heading to "rock bottom" and our subsequent acknowledgment of God. God, in His mercy, will introduce a crisis to accelerate the process. Instead of wasting 20 or 40 years of our lives before we finally acknowledge that God is God, the crisis gets us to that point in say, three to five years.

Our troubles are a wakeup call for us to pray and an opportunity for God to move on our behalf, but only if we pray. The greatness of the problem will determine the volume of our cry. You will experience some problem in your life, and you'll come to the point where you realize that the only way this *thing* will be resolved is if you pray about the matter. God is trying to get your attention. Conversely, He blesses you, and His favor, in return, must be acknowledged with authentic praise. Again, God wants your attention, and you're driven to your knees in admiration.

A CRISIS IS AN ACCELERATOR TO THE POSITION TO
WHICH WE WERE HEADING IN THE FIRST PLACE.

Take My People Higher

The year 2004 ended in despondency, but praise God, 2005 began with a vision—a vision about the significance of prayer and, more importantly, about His church (my church) becoming a house of prayer. Late-summer 2004, I began to attend a local congregation in support of a former classmate who had recently been baptized. She was traveling a great distance to attend church, and this congregation was within walking distance from her home. In private conversations with some of the members, I expressed my belief that the church was on the edge of something great.

On November 13, 2004, the opportunity presented itself, and I stood before the entire church body and told them that I had decided to transfer my membership to their church. I shared with them that I was convinced that God was getting ready to do something great—something special at that church. I further instructed the members to tell their friends—those who were taking up space at other churches—to come and be a part of something special.

As I write, I believe that that church is still struggling to embody that greatness. But God can't lie, and His Word will never return unto Him void (Isaiah 55:11). He will do what He said He will do. That church and others can become great and do special things for God as He prepares to gather His children home.

Growing up, my parents always made sure that we were dressed appropriately for church. As I grew older, "come as you are" took on new meaning; yet I respected God's house and those I may stand before and would dress "properly" for church, making my parents proud. However, on December 18, 2004, I attended church dressed casually (slacks and a shirt—no tie and jacket). Big mistake? Humanly speaking, yes; spiritually speaking, no. God will use you how He wants to use you when He wants to use you.

That Sabbath morning, I found myself busied with everything (diagnosing electrical problems, searching for light switches, etc.) but worship. As I continued with my activities in the church foyer, the head elder approached me. He informed me that the individual scheduled to lead the congregation in prayer was not coming and requested that I lead the congregation in prayer. While he was waiting on an answer, I was involved in a side conversation with the Holy Spirit about not being dressed and not being prepared.

The Holy Spirit said, "Tell him yes."

I said "Yes" and began worrying. *What do I say to the people? What do I pray about?* Before praying, as members shared their testimonies and prayer requests, I took notes—now I had something to pray about. The Holy Spirit caused me to pray like I can only remember doing one other time in my life. It was a sad, but true, commentary on my prayer life. When I returned to my seat, the Holy Spirit said to me, "If worship is a vertical experience, you have a responsibility to take my people higher."

The next day I meditated upon that statement and promised God and myself that I would never stand before His people without taking them higher. I also knew that if I were going to take His people higher, I, myself, had to go higher.

On December 25, 2004, I found myself sitting in the dark of my parents' living room—alone, angry, and crying. I had done nothing to deserve what had happened, so I was angry. A few days before, I had boarded a flight bound for Cleveland, Ohio, to spend the Christmas holiday with my family. This Christmas was the worst of my adult life—not because of the bitter cold and the lake-effect snow produced by Lake Erie, but because God was driving me to my knees.

I began to question whether I was fit to take God's people higher. *How can I take God's people higher when I'm so angry and want nothing to do with these people (specific family members)?* I was having this conversation with myself, but the Holy Spirit decided to join in, and He answered my question: "You must be about your Father's business." He went on to remind me that Jesus, while respectful, never stopped to explain, reason and/or apologize to His parents. Rather, He said unto them, "Why is it that you were looking for Me? Did you not know that I had to be in My Father's house?" (Luke 2:49, NASB). In other words, "Hugh, forget about this—*take My people higher!*"

IN THE MIDDLE OF THE STORM, WE'RE OFTEN
PRAYERLESS AND THUS POWERLESS.

In hindsight, I hold that Christmas dear because God was preparing me for something. At the time, I was completely unaware of what. But because of the way He sustained me, because of the way He comforted me, because of the way He revealed Himself, I now understand that He was in the midst all the time. When you're stuck in or going through the storm, it is hard to see or experience God's guidance or to feel His presence.

Listen to me, before the storm comes, we talk about "don't wait till the battle is over, shout now." At the end of the storm, we can't praise God enough. But in the middle of the storm, we're often prayerless and thus powerless.

In the midst of the storm that Christmas, somehow I found the strength to pray and cry. I was angry, but I was able to "sin not" (Ephesians 4:26, KJV). While praying and crying, God revealed Himself. While He never appeased me with an explanation, He simply told me I must be about my Father's business. Encouraged by God's clear voice, I determined that I must press on because God had something great He wanted me to do. He wanted me to take His people higher.

The Throne of Grace

I returned home, went back to work after the new year holiday, and found myself on the evening of January 7, 2005, preparing a sermon for the next time I was called on to preach. The phone rang, and a few friends were on the line. I made a call and added another friend to the conference call. We talked until 12:30 a.m. the next morning and ended our conversation, talking about the importance of prayer. One friend on the line had recently returned from attending a prayer meeting at Brooklyn Tabernacle in Brooklyn, New York, and the Holy Spirit was working with him as to this *thing* of prayer. He was convinced that we needed to pray more, and he wanted to share with us.

"Why wait? Hugh, we're coming over for lunch tomorrow," one bold friend said.

As directed, we had lunch and watched a DVD[2] of Jim Cymbala, the pastor of Brooklyn Tabernacle, preaching about the importance of God's house being a house of prayer. To close the sermon, he shared his testimony of how prayer became the standard when faced with a difficult situation—dealing with a rebellious daughter. During his sermon, he made the statement that "prayer takes us to the throne of grace." Hebrews 4:16, "Let us therefore come boldly unto the throne of grace that we may obtain mercy, and find grace to help in time of need."

That's it! "Higher" is to the throne of grace. The connection was made! The Holy Spirit had once again completed a successful mission. God had told me to take His people higher, and now He had revealed and confirmed where *higher* is. Moreover, He had revealed the means whereby it would occur. If worship is a vertical experience, you have a responsibility to take His people higher. Where is higher? It is the throne of grace. How do you get there? Prayer!

We're busy dawdling at the foot of the cross when Jesus is waiting for us at the throne of grace. Don't get me wrong; the foot of the cross is very important. The foot of the cross is where you humble yourself at the thought of what Jesus did for you at Calvary. The foot of the cross is where it begins, but you can't stay there. Jesus has ascended and is waiting for you at the throne of grace.

I had been charged with the responsibility to take God's people higher. And now I knew that higher was to the throne of grace and that the only way to get there was through prayer. In his book, *Unlocking Heaven's Storehouse*, George Vandeman emphasizes, "Prayer is a lifeline let down from the throne of grace."³

"My house shall be called a house of prayer." God's vision for all of His churches is that they become houses of prayer and for each member to use that lifeline to meet Him at the throne of grace. The throne of grace is where you will obtain mercy, access peace, find help, and receive what you need.

If you're looking for a job or a better job, it's at the throne of grace. Needing forgiveness? It's at the throne of grace. If you're looking for a spouse, he or she is at the throne of grace. Healing can be found at the throne of grace. Salvation, peace, love, guidance, hope, rest, protection, joy, comfort, patience, strength, discipline, and courage are all available at the throne of grace. If you're looking for wisdom, it is found at the throne of grace. Prosperity is at the throne of grace. You've got to go higher, and higher, and higher, and higher in prayer. "My house shall be called a house of prayer."

Casting the Vision

After watching the DVD, we continued to converse about prayer, shared our prayer requests, and pledged to pray intensely for each other over the next 30 days. I fell asleep that night praying and woke up praying the next morning, thanking God for what He had done and asking for His guidance and leadership in my life. The Holy Spirit began to show me how everything, since November 13, 2004, fit together and that I needed to share it. *But how?* My friends and I had decided to get together the next week to continue our discussion. The Holy Spirit said, "Hugh, call the pastor and invite him and the elders to lunch."

I was cautioned, however, to respect the pastor's authority and not to call anyone else at the church until I had spoken with him. I called the pastor, but he did not answer. I left him a message, called my friend who had shared the DVD, and told him what I had been impressed to do. I also called another friend and shared the lunch idea with her. We decided to fast and pray on Monday that the way would be opened for me to share God's vision for His church with others.

On January 10, 2005, I ended my fast at about 6:00 p.m. and went about my evening's activities. During that time, I missed a call from the pastor. He left me a message, thanking me for the invitation and shared that his mother was ill. Because of her condition, he was not sure if he would be in town, but that we would talk later. With my new understanding of the power of prayer, I started to pray for his mother. As I ended my prayer, the Holy Spirit said, "Hugh, call the head elder."

When I called, I asked, "Who is speaking on the Sabbath?"

He responded, "1 was hoping you would."

After speaking at length with the head elder about the growth and development of our church, I called my friend to let him know that the Lord had opened the way for me to cast the vision. He stopped me before I could say anything additional.

"You don't know this, but I was impressed that you should be the one to cast the vision, and I've been praying for that. Now, tell me what happened."

I told him that I would have the opportunity to cast the vision on Sabbath; we prayed and rejoiced together.

January 15, 2005, when the Holy Spirit allowed me to share my experience and re-introduce my church to prayer, marked the beginning of the journey to the throne of grace. I began my sermon that Sabbath with a quote from Oliver Wendell Holmes: "Man's mind, once stretched by a new idea, never again regains its original dimensions." I told the members that the Holy Spirit wanted to stretch their minds. While prayer itself is not a new idea, we corporately, as a church, have failed to fully understand its power. We say, "Much prayer, much power," but I don't think we really believe that precept.

A true understanding of the power that comes through prayer is a new idea to many believers. The Holy Spirit today wants to stretch your minds; it will never regain its original dimensions. I told the people that I wanted to spend our time together that afternoon talking about the power of prayer and the significance of a praying church. My goal was to lay the foundation for prayer's becoming the unquestioned heart and center of the church. I was honest with the congregation and told them that I wanted prayer to become so much a natural part of our church life that it is our first response to anything—not our last resort once everything else has been tried.

For the church of Jesus Christ, prayer is not a luxury, optional if we're not too busy, or what we do after we've exhausted every other option.

"Prayer is simply coming before the King of Heaven and asking. Prayer is not the same as talking to yourself, thinking positive thoughts, or wishing real hard. It is asking of God. The very fact that our God offers us an audience before his throne is reason enough for us to pray."[4]

On the first Sabbath in January, the head elder had outlined the services that we needed to provide to the community as a church. I took the opportunity, while casting the vision for prayer, to remind the members that the only way we would become a house of service was to first become a house of prayer. In his book, *The Praying Church Sourcebook*, Alvin J. Vander Griend notes, "Power for ministry can be released only through prayer."[5] Stop worrying and start praying; stop complaining and start praying; stop gossiping and start praying; stop stressing about who'll be the next pastor and start praying; stop thinking about the church office you didn't get and start praying. Stop and start praying.

THE ONLY WAY WE WOULD BECOME A HOUSE OF
SERVICE WAS FIRST TO BECOME A HOUSE OF PRAYER.

I was unapologetic in letting the congregation know that there was nothing special about them, the church, or me that God would decide to stop by our church as opposed to the church around the corner. The only difference was that this church was a house of prayer.

A Champion Is Born

As a result of a problem and His subsequent answer to your prayer or His unmerited favor, you become a believer in the power of prayer. When you become a believer in the power of prayer, you get the vision. You will ask yourself, *Will God move like this if I pray? Wow! Well, what if members of my family pray? Wait! What if my friends and everyone in my church prays?* My friend, you now have a clear vision of what can and will happen when you and others pray. "My house shall be called the house of prayer." When you get that vision, you become a champion—a champion of prayer is born for Christ.

If God's house (your church) is to become a house of prayer, God must have someone who will champion the cause. That someone must be someone who will cry out, "This house will become a house of prayer!" God does not need you, but being the kind of

God that He is, He's willing to include you in His plans to finish the work that He began with prayer (Acts 1:14). He did not need Noah to build the ark, Joseph to decode Pharaoh's dream, Moses to part the Red Sea, or Joshua to bring down the walls of Jericho. Though nothing was special about them, He was willing to use them.

WHEN YOU BECOME A BELIEVER IN THE POWER OF

PRAYER, YOU GET THE VISION.

No one prayed for the children of Israel like Moses did. Moses faced a situation that drove him to his knees. Rejected by Pharaoh and by Israel, he cried out to God:

"...Lord," he protested, "How can you mistreat your own people like this? Why did you ever send me if you were going to do this to them? Ever since I gave Pharaoh your message, he has only been more and more brutal to them, and you have not delivered them at all" (Exodus 5:22, 23, TLB).

When God responded to Moses by letting him know that He is the Lord and that He was going to do what He said He would do and subsequently sent ten plagues on Egypt, Moses became a champion of prayer.

So when faced with the Red-Sea situation, Moses did what a prayer champion would do—he prayed. Moses is standing at the Red Sea; Pharaoh's army is behind him, the Red Sea is in front of him, steep cliffs on each side. What do you do? You have to pray. As a result of that prayer, God said to him: "Raise your staff and stretch out your hand over the sea to divide the water" (Exodus 14:16, NIV). Moses' experience drove him to his knees, and some experience will likewise drive you to your knees.

I find it curious that God would determine, at this point, to involve Moses. God could easily have parted the Red Sea with His hands, but He did not. Why? Because He had a prayer champion whom He wanted to use. God does not contract with a prayer champion to use him/her. He uses the prayer champion because He wants to, and He wants to because every time you're involved in answered prayer, it sets the stage for more prayer and results in more answered prayer. Consequently, you develop a profound understanding of the importance and significance of prayer. Prayer becomes the unquestioned heart and center of your life.

When you realize the power of prayer and make yourself available to be used by God, He will help you to embody the vision and use you to bring about change in the lives of others through your prayers.

Congratulations, you're now on your way to making some church a house of prayer. Remember, however, that nothing is special about you. God does not need you, but He is willing to use you.

Casting the Vision: Part II

Nearly six months later after preaching additional sermons on prayer, the Holy Spirit took me back to Matthew 21, and He began to reveal, step-by-step, the process whereby a church would become a house of prayer. With that new insight, I stood before the church in mid-June 2005 and preached *God's Vision: A House of Prayer II.* I was candid with the congregation that afternoon and told them that, at the outset, I honestly had no understanding of where the Lord was leading me or how He was going to accomplish His charge to me: "Hugh, take My people higher." Over the last few months, however, being the God that He is, He had revealed to me step-by-step, moment-by-moment, prayer-by-prayer, how He intended to make our church a house of prayer.

I acknowledged to the congregation that a fuller understanding of prayer had stretched my mind, and I knew that their minds had also been stretched. I told them it would have been virtually impossible to have regularly attended this church over the past few months and maintained their current way of thinking about prayer. I used the word *virtually* because I knew that some of them were trying their best to defy the laws of nature by retooling their minds to their original dimensions. I reminded them, however, that doing so was impossible.

In addition, I took the opportunity to recap what I had shared with them in January, i.e., that prayer is the activity that takes us to the throne of grace—that the action as it relates to prayer is at the throne of grace. At the throne of grace is where we'll obtain mercy and find grace to help in our time of need. The only way to get to the throne of grace is through prayer.

Revisiting these concepts was important because over the last few weeks leading up to this sermon, I'd been approached with questions like: "When are we going to move on to something else?" "Where are we going next?" "What about the other ministries of the church?" I provided a collective response: "To those who are questioning where we're going and the means by which we're going to get there, let me be clear this afternoon in saying that we're going to the throne of grace because that's where the action is. Prayer is the only vehicle that will get us there."

With the understanding that the tremendous power for ministry can only be released through prayer, it was my hope that we, as a church, would be sold-out to prayer. Instead, a few individuals—not many, only a few—were defiant to God's warnings and were causing others to grumble and complain.

In spite of the naysayers, you have to move forward! You must make your church a house of prayer. Prayer must become the foundation, walls, and roof of your church. Without a foundation and a covering of prayer and without prayer as the thread binding your church together, everything you do—every activity, every program, every ministry—will fail, fold, or fall.

One Accord

Get this: the word "symphony" comes from the word *accord*. A symphony is different instruments, all playing the same score to produce a harmonious union of sounds. Prayer, i.e. harmony in prayer, is the only thing that will bring about single purpose in mind, singleness of heart, a symphony—one accord. Any church (the different members), all on the same page spiritually (through prayer), results in awesome power to save souls. The church is God's appointed agency for the salvation of men. Furthermore, the members are to find their happiness in the happiness of those whom they help and bless.[6] Accordingly, our contemporary "Day of Pentecost" must come.

The day must come when we become a power-filled church where hundreds, thousands of souls are saved daily. But it cannot happen; it will not happen until we develop spiritual unity by first becoming a house of prayer. We cannot receive the full blessing God is ready to bestow through His Spirit until we seek and receive it in fellowship with each other.[7] What is our ultimate goal as a church—our mission? The only way we will fulfill our mission and our goal is that the Holy Spirit moves us. And the only way the Holy Spirit (the latter rain) will fall is for us to be in one accord. How do we get to be in one accord?

Bible studies? No.

Healthy eating? No.

Music? No.

Preaching? No.

Community service? No.

Fellowship dinners? No.

Understand me, God can and will use all these ministries, but somebody, somewhere has to be praying. He never said my house shall be called a house of Bible study. Our churches were intended to be and should be houses of prayer. No ministry will give us single purpose in mind. No ministry will achieve singleness of heart. No ministry will bind us in one accord, spiritually. The only way for any organization or church to be in one accord spiritually is if all are praying. Prayer is the only thing that can attach us, all at once, to Jesus.

When we're praying, we all must acknowledge His sovereignty. Prayer is the only thing that levels the playing field. God does not care if you have a GED or an MD. He does not care if you're 4 or 84 years old. God does not care if you work in the mailroom or boardroom. He does not care if you're black or white. God does not care if you make minimum wage or six figures. He does not care if you live in a one-bedroom apartment or a million-dollar mansion. God does not care! At His feet, we're all equally poor or rich.

PRAYER IS THE ONLY THING THAT CAN ATTACH US,

ALL AT ONCE, TO JESUS.

He never said, "I live to make the choir sound good, to grow the marriage club, to ensure that all are vegetarians.' Listen to me, He said, "I live; I sit on the right hand of the Father to make intercession for you" (Hebrews 7:25). That is prayer! That is currently His main purpose for being. If Jesus sees one of His primary roles as praying, how much more should prayer and praying be a fundamental part of our lives. Prayer is the only thing that ties us to Him equally without any prerequisites. "My house," God declares; my temple; my church; my sanctuary…whatever you prefer to call it. My house shall be called a house of prayer. Get the vision!

You must ask yourself: Have I embodied the vision? If you have not embodied the vision, if you have not said I now know, I now understand the power of prayer; you have to go back. If you have, however, grasped the magnitude and importance of prayer—you're ready to move forward.

Reflections

_____

_____

_____

_____

_____

_____

_____

_____

_____

_____

_____

_____

_____

Notes

1   Bob Sorge, *The Fire of Delayed Answers: Are You Waiting for Your Prayers to Be Answered?* (Kansas City, Mo.: Oasis House, 2008), p. 9.

2   Link to video—*www.youtube.com/watch?v=40F5wMbjugE*

3   George Vandeman, *Unlocking Heaven's Storehouse* (Thousand Oaks, Calif.: It Is Written, 1980), p. 9.

4   *http://www.sermoncentral.com/sermons/first-of-all-pray-roger-thomas-sermon-on-prayer-adoration-68971.asp?Page=1*

5   Alvin J. Vander Griend, *The Praying Church Sourcebook* (Grand Rapids: Church Development Resources, 1990), p. 4.

6   Ellen G. White, *Acts of the Apostles: In the Proclamation of the Gospel of Jesus Christ* (Omaha, Neb.: Pacific Press Publishing Association, 1911), pp. 9, 12.

7   Andrew Murray, *Andrew Murray on Prayer* (New Kensington, Penn.: Whitaker House, 1998), p. 380.

TWO

Spiritual Robbers

Jesus entered the temple courts and drove out
all who were buying and selling there. He overturned
the tables of the moneychangers and the benches of those
selling doves.... [13] but you are making it a "den of robbers."

—Matthew 21:12, 13 (NIV)

I f you've embodied the vision, then you're ready to begin the
process of *prayerfully* removing what I call spiritual robbers from
your church. This is the *second* phase (see Figure 3) in becoming
a house of prayer. Note that I used the word *begin*. Praying for the
removal of spiritual robbers is not a one-time, but rather, a lifetime
activity. If your church is to become and remain a house of prayer,
you'll have to engage spiritual robbers, through prayer, on a regular
basis. In a world of sacred and secular, the adjective *spiritual* would
appear to be a peculiar descriptor of the noun *robber*. However,

there is no other way to describe these individuals, practices, and/ or things that rob God of His glory.

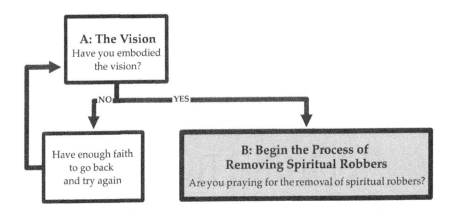

Figure 3. Removing Spiritual Robbers

In Trouble, Again

As the questions persisted about "when we would be moving to something other than prayer," about "where are we going to go next," and about "equal time for the other ministries of the church," it became reasonably obvious to me that there were members or groups of members that were intent on preventing our church from becoming a house of prayer. Subsequently, the Holy Spirit clearly showed me that these individuals were spiritual robbers and that they needed to be *prayerfully* removed from His house.

Please keep in mind that the removal could be physical. Conversely, it could be a removal of the individual's cantankerous and rebellious nature. We need to acknowledge that "an enemy hath done this" (Matthew 13:28, KJV) and that we're obligated to respond. We cannot sit back and do nothing while spiritual robbers take over our churches. I'm asking you to pray, and God will do the rest. Understand that I'm not asking you to make any decisions about or keep any list of whom or what should go or stay; I'm asking you to pray.

Foremost, please note that this battle of removing spiritual robbers is a divine battle—not a physical one. However, as I have already noted, there is a physical element to it if you read John's description of this confrontation. Jesus, Himself, fashioned a whip and went into the temple (John 2:15). I'm not asking anyone to take action like that! For us, it's a spiritual battle. What I am asking you to do is to *prayerfully* drive out the spiritual robbers that are bent on preventing God's house from becoming a house of prayer. I'm going to get into trouble; but then, I often do when I speak to the practical application of this passage. But it's not me; I'm reading from the Bible.

Jesus had to come along and clear the temple because the priests, teachers, and leaders allowed reprehensible behavior (the buying and selling in the temple) to continue unregulated and unchecked. They had made the very symbols pointing to the Lamb of God a means to ill gotten, personal gain. Let me be very clear, if there is any individual, practice, and/or thing that is preventing your church from becoming a house of prayer, it is a spiritual robber and must be driven from, thrown down, or chased out before that which is right can be established. Someone, or something, has to go.

"To gain that which is worth having, it may be necessary to lose everything else."[1] As such, temple clearing is a difficult, painful process for many because sometimes it involves our own family members and personal things. To engage in kingdom building with Christ, you may have to leave behind your home, brother, sister, father, mother, wife, husband, children, or property (Matthew 19:29). Occasionally, there is not enough room for Christ and some individuals or some things in our lives. Likewise, there may not be enough room for spiritual robbers and Christ in our churches. When God shows up, something or someone has to give way.

Strange Math

Please understand that this move by Jesus to drive out the spiritual robbers was not the act of a coward or some evil person. The same Jesus who turned water into wine, who healed leprosy, who calmed the raging sea, who caused the blind to see, who fed five thousand, who raised the dead to life, who caused the lame to walk, carried out an act of love. He is loving, kind, forgiving, and merciful. Yet God is not weak or accommodating toward those who prevent His house from becoming a house of prayer. Some subtraction must occur for the kingdom of God to be multiplied.

Strange math, but true—a difficult concept, but biblical. There is precedent in scripture for this concept of the *eventual* separation of sacred from secular and the Godly from the ungodly for the benefit of the whole.

"We are in the shaking time, the time when everything that can be shaken will be shaken. The Lord will not excuse those who know the truth if they do not in word and deed obey His commands. If we make no effort to win souls to Christ we shall be held responsible for the work we might have done, but did not do because of our spiritual indolence."[2]

Some subtraction must occur for the kingdom of God to be multiplied.

Read the parable of the wheat and tares in Matthew 13:24-30 and about the lukewarm state of the church in Revelation 3:14-16. Both passages provide an illustration of the process whereby the righteous is separated from the unrighteous—those who refuse to accept Christ as Lord. All those who live their lives in such a way as to deny the superiority of Christ cannot and will not forever be connected to Him or His church. A time will come when these spiritual robbers will be gathered, bundled, and burned, or they will be spewed out of His mouth. If we pray, in time, God will disconnect Himself and His church from those with their own agendas and motives.

Matthew 13:30 says, "Let both grow together until the harvest...." The wheat and the tares were allowed to grow together until the harvest because of the inability to distinguish them from each other during the period of continued growth. In many of our churches, however, there is a well-defined difference between those who are fostering the development of the church and those who are hindering said development. We're able to "...discern between the righteous and the wicked, between him that serveth God and him that serveth him not (Malachi 3:18, KJV). The tremendous difference between the wheat and tares must be addressed spiritually and prayerfully.

E. M. Bounds states:

> "Blessed is that church that has praying leaders who can see what is disorderly in the church, who are grieved about it, and who put forth their hands to correct the evils that harm God's cause as a weight to its progress."[3]

He continues:

> "...there was the desired objective of riddance from men who were hurtful to the church of God and who were a hindrance to the running of the Word of the Lord. Let us ask, are there not in the present-day church those who are a definite hindrance to the ongoing of the Word of the Lord? What seems to be harsh is actually obedience to God, is for the welfare of the church, and is wise in the extreme."[4]

As I further considered this topic of the removal of spiritual robbers, I was reminded of the extended and preventable journey of the Israelites.

"The Israelites had moved about in the wilderness forty years until all the men who were of military age when they left Egypt had died, since they had not obeyed the Lord. For the Lord had sworn to them that they would not see the land he had solemnly promised their ancestors to give us, a land flowing with milk and honey" (Joshua 5:6, NIV).

Before His people could enter the Promised Land, God had to eliminate an entire generation because of their disobedience. Again, God's removal of those who are disobedient and hindering the progress of His people and work is not uncommon. God will not allow anyone to hold Him, His people, or His work hostage. It does not matter if it takes forty days or forty years, keep praying; God will remove spiritual robbers. Don't allow spiritual robbers to prevent your church from reaching its Promised Land in a timely fashion. Some subtraction must occur for the kingdom of God to be multiplied.

GOD WILL NOT ALLOW ANYONE TO HOLD HIM,
HIS PEOPLE, OR HIS WORK HOSTAGE.

The process of targeted removal to enhance growth and productivity of the whole is biblical. *Pruning* is part of the horticultural process whereby superfluous and unwanted parts of a tree are removed. In this process, the gardener removes dead or overgrown branches and stems to increase the fruitfulness and growth of the tree. "He cuts off every branch of mine that doesn't produce fruit, and he prunes the branches that do bear fruit so they will produce even more" (John 15:2, NLT).

Spiritual robbers will be pruned—cut off—from God's church because they are superfluous and unwanted. Why? Because they are not bearing fruit. Their weekly attendance at church and related activities do nothing to advance the church. These *branches* (church members) targeted for pruning are dead and overgrown. They are taking up space, sapping energy, and are crowding out the sun (Son)—the free-flowing light that is necessary for the growth and production of the tree (church). This light from the Son is the primary way in which churches derive their energy. Absent this light, and churches will not grow and produce. Consequently, the gardener (Christ) must prune to remove spiritual robbers.

At some point, you'll have to clear the room. Mark 5:35-43 tells the story of Jesus on His way to Jairus' home to heal his daughter. The house was crowded with mourners when Jesus got there. He told them she was not dead, but sleeping. The crowd laughed at Him, and He cleared the room. It is often hard to get to those in need when some individuals around you are not well-intentioned. Your faith gives you a different perspective; "She is not dead," but all you hear is laughter. Sometimes, you'll have to clear the room of spiritual robbers (those who are laughing because of their lack of faith) to get to those in need of healing. Some subtraction must occur for the kingdom of God to be multiplied.

"When hypocrites and the half-hearted can dwell in our midst without being convicted or made uncomfortable, then something's wrong. God intends for His fire to so envelope the local church that hypocrites will not be able to stay, and the devout will not be able to remain unchanged."[5]

I'm not asking anyone to physically set his church on fire, but church members need, through prayer, to set it ablaze. *Prayerfully* ignite an inferno of God's purifying fire that will make spiritual robbers uncomfortable to the point that they're willing to leave or change their behavior; simply pray.

Spiritual Robbers

Some of you are saying car and jewelry thieves, I know. Who or what are spiritual robbers? Spiritual robbers are 1) any individual, practice, and/or thing that robs God of His honor and glory, 2) any individual, practice, and/or thing that robs church visitors and members of the knowledge, character, and requirements of God, and 3) any individual, practice, and/or thing that robs visitors and non-members alike of the opportunity to know and accept Christ as their personal Savior.

You must ask yourself this question: does this person, this practice, this activity, this program, this ministry lend itself to making my church a house of prayer? If the answer is no, it must be driven out and/or renounced. Individuals, practices, and/or things who are doing zilch to promote a house of prayer must go. Anything or anyone who causes a church to be distracted from prayer is a spiritual robber. Anyone or anything you bring into God's house that does not support His house becoming a house of prayer must be uprooted.

It has been said that the church is a hospital for the "sin-sick soul," and I agree with that statement. But at some point, the *terminally* ill are sent home or to hospice to die. In other words, we, as loving members, must and will work with that individual to bring him/her to an understanding of right and wrong—a place of spiritual correctness. But when enough is enough, a void must be created to allow God's Spirit to reign and operate; somebody or something has to go! I don't mean to sound harsh, to appear uncaring, or any harm, but we can no longer play games with each other. Sometimes a breakaway is a breakthrough.

Too many churches want to be counted among the mega-churches and allow any and everything while trying to maintain their status. At times, they lose members and become discouraged for the wrong reasons. They're playing the "numbers game."

"There is such a lust for members in the church in these modern times, that the officials and preachers have entirely lost sight of the members who have violated baptismal covenants and who are living in open disregard of God's Word. The idea now is quantity in membership, not quality. The purity of the church is put in the background in the craze to secure numbers, to pad the church rolls, and to make large figures in statistical columns."[6]

I'm completely convinced that God will hold us responsible for not *prayerfully* removing those who refuse to make His house a house of prayer. Similarly, He will hold us responsible for allowing His house to be used for any and everything while we ignore prayer. As such, if I have to, I'm willing to err on the side of God. I'm going to, and I'm asking you to take your chances with God; you'll never lose.

Again, please know that I am not asking you to make any decisions about or keep any list of whom or what should go or stay; I am only asking you to pray. Mark 9:29 is clear: "This kind can be cast out only by prayer." I want you to *prayerfully* drive out the spiritual robbers who are bent on preventing God's house from becoming a house of prayer. This is a spiritual battle—not a physical one. You will, however, be held responsible for not joining forces with God.

Double Agent

Note in Matthew 21:12 that not only the "sellers," but also the "buyers" were driven out of the temple. You cannot sit around and say, "I had nothing to do with it—I'm just here." My friend, if you're not part of the solution, you're a part of the problem. No organization can advance if individuals, practices, and/or things are holding it back. If you're not working with the leadership of your church to establish a house of prayer, you're as guilty as those who are working against the leadership. The buyers and the sellers alike were chased out of the temple.

IF YOU PLAY BOTH SIDES, THE DEVIL WILL ABANDON YOU, AND GOD WILL DENY YOU.

Jesus says you are making it (the church) a den of robbers, a hangout for thieves (Matthew 21:13). God's house, the church—your church—cannot be the den, the hangout for *practicing* thieves (former thieves, yes; practicing thieves, no) and a house of prayer at the same time. Anything with two heads is seldom found moving forward with mutual consent. It's generally either moving sideways or backward. If such a being can be found moving forward in the same direction, it's usually with a tussle. Such struggling, however, cannot and should not exemplify the true Christian church.

Light and darkness cannot co-exist; oil and water will never mix. You are either hot or cold. You cannot serve two masters. "...Choose you this day whom ye will serve..." (Joshua 24:15, KJV). You can't sit on the fence when it comes to spiritual matters; you can't play both sides. Keep in mind that when double agents are caught, both sides usually deny any involvement with the agent. If you play both sides, the Devil will abandon you, and God will deny you.

Ask yourself: why would Jesus say in Matthew 21:13 that robbers were hiding-out in the temple? While it appears from Matthew 21:12 that Christ was simply throwing out merchants and their customers (buyers and sellers), in actuality He was chasing out robbers. Both merchants and customers were spiritual robbers. Had Jesus allowed the behavior of the merchants and their customers to go unchecked, the temple would have become a shopping mall. Sin unchecked will consume you; it will take over your life. If you don't purpose to make God's church a house of prayer, spiritual robbers will consume the church for their own gain. It will become their den, their hideout, and their hangout.

I will not, and I encourage you not to sit back and allow your church to become a hangout for practicing thieves—former thieves, yes, but not a hideout for individuals who have no intent on making His house a house of prayer.

Who or what is consuming your time that you can't pray? We cannot develop spiritually if certain matters in our lives are crowding out Jesus. Do you agree? So then, why would you expect a church to flourish and grow if certain things in the church are crowding out Jesus? While it pained God that He had to cast Lucifer out of heaven, He had to do it; He had no choice.

Every solution implemented is likely to cause a problem for someone. Know, however, that innovative solutions are disruptive and creative solutions are destructive. In much the same way, the spiritual solution of prayer is equally disruptive and destructive.

Some subtraction must occur for the kingdom of God to be multiplied. Spiritual robbers/thieves among us must be driven out to create a void that must be filled with champions of prayer and individuals in need of healing.

I've Prayed for You

I want to close this chapter by clearly illustrating the importance of praying for spiritual robbers. As the last supper was ending, Jesus took the opportunity to warn His disciples, namely Peter, about their unfaithfulness to Him.

"And the Lord said, Simon, Simon, behold, Satan hath desired to have you, that he may sift you as wheat: But I have prayed for thee, that thy faith fail not: and when thou art converted, strengthen thy brethren" (Luke 22:31, 32, KJV).

Sifting is "the process of separating something, especially something to be discarded, from something else." Spiritual robbers operate in this manner; their desire is to separate us from prayer and God. Their desire is for churches to discard prayer and God. Bottom line, the Devil's desire is to separate us from prayer and God. As such, he will attempt to use others, practices and/or things (spiritual robbers) in your church to sift you—to separate you from prayer and God.

But what did Jesus say to Peter? "I've prayed for you." We must do the same for the spiritual robbers in our churches. When spiritual robbers attempt to sift us—separate us from prayer and God—we must pray for them. Knowing what Peter was about to do, Jesus could have responded by attacking him or calling a committee meeting to discuss the situation. But He simply said, "...I've prayed for you." Wow!

With prayer comes strength to change the very spiritual nature of the spiritual robber. Jesus was confident in what Peter would become because of His prayer. As such, He said to him, "...when you're converted, strengthen your brother." We, likewise, must pray for our brothers and sisters that they don't allow themselves to be used by the Devil as spiritual robbers. Your conversion and subsequent prayers strengthens them; their conversion strengthens others. And thus, we begin the life-changing process of transforming the present culture of sifting (separating others from prayer and God) perpetrated by spiritual robbers in some of our churches.

Now, you must ask yourself: am I praying for the removal of spiritual robbers from my church? If your answer is "No," you have to go back and try again. If you are, however, you're ready to move forward.

Reflections

Reflections

Notes

1   Bernadette Devlin, *The Price of My Soul* (London: Pan Books Ltd, 1969), preface.

2   Ellen G. White, *The Colporteur Evangelist* (Omaha: Pacific Press Publishing Association, 1950), p. 25.

3   E. M. Bounds, *E. M. Bounds on Prayer* (New Kensington, Penn.: Whitaker House, 1997), p. 358.

4   Ibid, pp. 359–60.

5   Sorge, p. 15.

6   Bounds, p. 357.

THREE

The Proclamation

"It is written," he said to them,
"My house will be called a house of prayer…."

—Matthew 21:13 (NIV)

If you are in the process of praying for the removal of spiritual robbers from your church, then you are ready to proclaim God's house (your church), a house of prayer. This is the *third* phase (see Figure 4) in becoming a house of prayer. Jesus was explicit in His proclamation, and we must do the same. The house of prayer proclamation has its roots in the vision. With the awareness of the worth and influence of prayer, you'll purpose in your heart to make your church a house of prayer. Your church becoming a house of prayer is the reality, and this reality becomes your progressive objective. As such, you cannot help but make the proclamation.

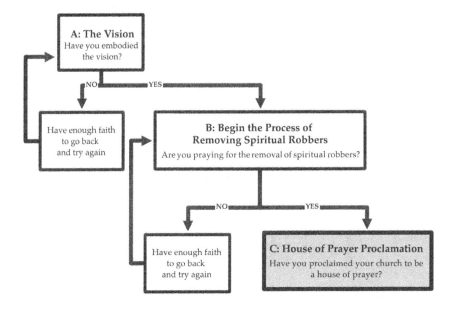

Figure 4. The Proclamation

The Standard

What if you were seeking a mechanic shop to repair your car and when you walked in, you found the mechanic making bread? Would you leave your car there? Similarly, what if you were in need of medical attention and were seeking a hospital? However, when you walked in, you discovered that it was a grocery store. Would you get in line? From all outward appearances, these establishments looked like what you were seeking. Moreover, the signs displayed on the buildings indicated a mechanic's shop and a hospital. Why would you not expect to find cars being fixed and medical services being provided?

In a similar way, our communities are seeking for God and prayer. From all outward appearances, our churches look like what they're seeking and the sign outside does use the word *church*. Why should they not expect to find Christ and prayer in our churches? After all, our churches are supposed to be houses of prayer. However, when those in need show up, they find everything else but Christ and find us doing everything else but praying. Accordingly, most of our communities and members are confused. Why would you expect them to stay? Why would *you* stay?

I'm in full agreement that "any church that calls itself the house of God but fails to magnify and teach the great lesson of prayer, should change its teaching to conform to the divine prayer pattern; or it should change the name of its building to something other than a church."[1] In other words, if you're not going to be a house of prayer, take down the church sign. Stop confusing your members and the community.

The house of prayer proclamation is setting and implementing prayer as the standard for your church. Prayer becomes the standard by which other churches measure themselves to you. Your church becomes the benchmark for all things prayer, and you're proud to say it. This, *prayer*, is what we do, and this is how we do it. First and most important, let your congregation know. Then let your surrounding community know what you stand for, and then let the world know. Include prayer in your mission and vision statements and make it the focus of your branding. The distinguishing feature—the defining mark of our churches—must be prayer.

Someone—the preacher, teacher, adult, or child—has to proclaim it loud and wide. The psychology behind verbalizing your church's position related to prayer is that someone heard you say it and will hold you accountable. Someone from your community—a visitor or even one of your members—may challenge you to honor your word. Once we say we're a house of prayer, we'll now have to uphold the declaration. As a result, many churches avoid making the proclamation because they don't want to be held accountable. Too often we have dreams, make plans, and then keep them to ourselves. If no one knows, then no one knows that I'm procrastinating or that I've failed. When we proclaim it, we authorize those hearers to hold us responsible. Someone will ask the preacher, teacher, adult, or child, "Did you not say that your church is a house of prayer?"

Labeling Your Church

Labeling theory is a theory associated with deviant behavior. An official label that tags a person as delinquent, for example, may have serious consequences for further deviation...as others react toward the individual in a manner consistent with that status.[2] In other words, we're a product of our labels; we become who others say we are. I often use the following example when I explain this theory to my students.

A nine-year-old boy, Dixon, steals a $1.75 bag of potato chips from the store. While this was Dixon's first time stealing, the shop owner called the police because he wanted to teach Dixon a lesson and send a message to the other children in the neighborhood. Weeks later, Dixon appears in juvenile court and is sentenced to community service; he's labeled a delinquent. The label did not go unrecognized by his parents, siblings, classmates, school administrators, and even church leaders. All of these individuals began to interact differently with Dixon because of the delinquent label; they treated him as if he was a thief. Several months later, Dixon stole a toy SUV truck from the local department store. Dixon is now 23 years old and his risk-taking behavior has increased; he has fully embraced the label. The self-fulfilling prophecy has occurred; Dixon became a product of the *delinquent* label some 14 years ago.

What's my point with this story? Perhaps you are wondering what labeling theory has to do with the proclamation? The answer? Everything! Spiritual leaders, label your church a house of prayer. Remember, according to labeling theory, we're a product of our labels; we become who others say we are. As Dixon was labeled a delinquent, label your church "a house of prayer." As already noted, proclaim it loud and wide. Encourage your departmental leaders, members and visitors to use the label: "house of prayer." Labeling your church a house of prayer is proclaiming it to be such. In time, through focused effort and prayer the congregation will become a product of the label.

MANY CHURCHES AVOID MAKING THE
PROCLAMATION BECAUSE THEY
DON'T WANT TO BE HELD ACCOUNTABLE.

The self-fulfilling prophecy will occur. Your departmental leaders, members and visitors will begin to treat the church like a house of prayer and will internalize the concept of being a place where prayer is a priority. You should know that the idea of this theory can and does apply to all facets of a church. Namely, if you label your church a house of preaching, house of music, or house of fellowship, it will become a house of preaching, music, and/or fellowship. Proclaim (label) your church what you want it to be—a house of prayer—and the church will become a product of that label.

When you make the proclamation that your church will become a house of prayer, know that nothing magical or paranormal will happen. You will not hear choirs singing, and bright lights will not fill the sky. What the proclamation does, however, is set in motion a chain of spiritual events that will bring power to your church. The foundation for power in your church is the proclamation. Figure 5 illustrates the sequence: the proclamation leads to more prayer, more prayer leads to one accord, one accord leads to the manifestation of the Holy Spirit, and the Holy Spirit brings power to the church. This is where the supernatural, not magical, power of God takes over.

Figure 5. The Proclamation Sequence

Power from Proclamation

In the next chapter, I will address how a church can tap into this available power—through prayer—to enable it and to develop and implement fruitful ministries to provide spiritual, physical, social, and emotional healing. The current question, however, is: how does a person get that needed power to effect healing? The only way for us to get healing power is through the outpouring of the Holy Spirit. The only means for us to witness the workings of the Holy Spirit is through being in one accord. And the only way for us to be in one accord is for us to become a house of prayer.

Consequently, when we make becoming a house of prayer (God's original plan for His temple) our solitary, spiritual objective, we will proclaim it boldly. That proclamation leads to more prayer, which brings one accord, and being in one accord will lead to an unthinkable familiarity with the Holy Spirit. And when the Holy Spirit is come, He provides awesome healing power.

Know that, "God is pleased to answer individual prayers, but at times He seems to say, you may entreat my favor, but I will not see your face unless your brethren are with you."[3] When it comes to spiritual matters, we cannot simply agree to disagree. This agreement will not produce the one accord needed to unleash power. What I'm saying to you is this: if we don't become a house of prayer, we will never be on the same page spiritually. And if we're not on the same page spiritually, we will never have the necessary power to bring about desired change in our churches and communities.

The book of Acts illustrates the type of power that can be unleashed through prayer. Allow me to demonstrate.

a. *Before the day of Pentecost:* "The apostles often met together and prayed with a single purpose in mind. The women and Mary the mother of Jesus would meet with them, and so would his brothers" (Acts 1:14, CEV). If you missed it, the first organized meeting of the early church was a prayer meeting. This meeting was in sharp contrast to the competitive spirit witnessed among the disciples at the Last Supper.

They "often met together." Prayer must be done often and done together. If we're trying to develop one accord in anticipation of the Holy Spirit, prayer can't be a casual activity in which we engage when we have some free time. Accordingly, we must have a "single purpose in mind" (one accord), and that purpose must be preparing ourselves for the reception of and fellowship with the Holy Spirit to receive the necessary power to bring about desired change in our churches and communities. In summary, notice that being both "often in prayer" and in an attitude of "single purpose" took place before the day of Pentecost. This is the type of praying and unity that must characterize the current church as we spiritually await the manifestation of God's power in these last days.

b. *On the day of Pentecost:* "When the day of Pentecost came; they were all together in one place. All of them were filled with the Holy Spirit and began to speak in other languages as the Spirit enabled them" (Acts 2:1, 2:4, NIV). "When the day of Pentecost came"—not *if*, but *when*. Jesus has promised that the Holy Spirit would be poured out, allowing us to do great and wonderful works, and we would receive power (Acts 1:8). The latter rain is coming; there is no question about that—God said it, and He can't lie. The question is: are we ready to receive it?

I submit to you that we've been praying an incomplete prayer. In addition to praying for the Holy Spirit to come, our prayer must also include: "Lord, prepare me (us) to receive the Holy Spirit." The passage is silent as to whether or not the disciples were in prayer *on* the day of Pentecost, but I can only imagine that they were still praying when the Holy Spirit descended. In summary, "praying" and "being in one accord" on the day of Pentecost allowed the promised Holy Spirit to fall and enabled mighty works.

c. *After Pentecost:* "And they, continuing daily with one accord in the temple, and breaking bread from house to house, did eat their meat with gladness and singleness of heart. Praising God, and having favor with all the people. And the Lord added to the church daily such as should be saved" (Acts 2:46, 47, KJV). "They continued daily." Praying and developing one accord is not a one-time occurrence. You can't get tired of praying and be ready to move on to something else.

HAVE IT AND USE IT; USE IT AND HAVE MORE OF IT.

"Hearing the report, they lifted their voices in a wonderful harmony in prayer. While they were praying, the place where they were meeting trembled and shook. They were all filled with the Holy Spirit and continued to speak God's Word with fearless confidence" (Acts 4:24, 31, MSG). As a result of continued prayer, the place was shaken, and they were filled with the Holy Spirit for a second time. In addition, they preached the word with boldness. Had the disciples not appropriately used the first outpouring, the second would not have come. Have it and use it; use it and have more of it.

Finally, "And through the hands of the apostles many signs and wonders were done among the people. And they were all with one accord in Solomon's Porch. And believers were increasingly added to the Lord, multitudes of both men and women" (Acts 5:12, 14, NKJV). Too often we try to make it hard, but the formula is very simple—proclamation, prayer, one accord, Holy Spirit, power! I can't say it enough or any clearer: the proclamation leads to prayer, prayer brings one accord, one accord positions us for the outpouring of the Holy Spirit, and when the Holy Spirit is come, He provides power to complete the work. If we don't proclaim our churches to be houses of prayer, we will never be able to tap into the available power that will enable us to provide spiritual, physical, social, and emotional healing as the disciples did in the early church.

That We May Be One

In John 17:21 (KJV) Jesus prays, "That they all may be one; as thou, Father, art in me, and I in thee, that they also may be one in us: that the world may believe that thou hast sent me." In this passage, Christ is praying that we will be one, though not one in everything. This is neither possible nor required; rather, He was praying to be one in the great things of God, i.e., oneness in spirit and in spiritual objectives, beliefs, aims, and desires. In praying this prayer, Jesus was confident that if oneness happened, the world would then believe in Him.

Sounds simple enough, right? And it is. You and I, however, continue to be the problem. Ellen G. White had the following to say:

"It's not the opposition of the world that most endangers the church of Christ. It is the evil cherished in the hearts of believers... on the other hand, the strongest witness that God has sent His Son into the world is the existence of harmony and union among men of varied dispositions who form His church."[4]

If you're following me, you understand the importance of what Jesus prayed for and why. In other words, you recognize what needs to happen for this world to believe. Furthermore, I hope you can also now appreciate my analysis and conclusion that we're the problem. And so, the question remains: how do we become one, thereby allowing the world to believe? Many diversity and inclusion strategies attempt to achieve unity in our society. However, one component is missing from those strategies, and that missing ingredient is prayer for and with each other.

Praying for and with each other is the best inclusion approach; it leads to oneness, which results in the manifestation of the Holy Spirit and produces belief. If you've never connected John 17:21 to Acts 1:14, 2:1, 4, and 41, allow me to do so forthwith. What is the relationship? Stick with me; I'm going somewhere. A few days before His crucifixion, Jesus prayed. The key word here is *prayed*—asking that we become one. He knew that oneness would lead to belief, and the world would believe.

By the time we get to Acts 1:14 and Acts 2:1, you'll recognize that Jesus' prayer is already being answered. Acts 1:14 (KJV) reads, "These all continued with one accord in prayer and supplication, with the women, and Mary the mother of Jesus, and with his brethren." Acts 2:1 (KJV) continues, "And when the day of Pentecost was fully come, they were all with one accord in one place." In great contrast to the sometimes dysfunctional relationship we witnessed between the disciples prior to the cross, there is now one accord—oneness.

How did this being in one accord happen? The answer? The prayer of Jesus. How is oneness likely to continue today? The answer? The prayers of modern-day disciples. Oneness that produces belief cannot and will not occur without prayer. Someone (Jesus) had to pray for it to begin, and those who are to be one (you and I) must pray for and with each other if it is to continue. I want you to understand that prayer produces oneness in our lives that will impress and inspire this world. Whatever interferes with this accord must be removed, or it will prevent your church from becoming a house of prayer. Churches and their members who are in the best frame of mind to receive spiritual blessings are in a praying frame of mind.[5]

IF YOU WANT TO DEVELOP ONENESS THAT WILL
CAUSE THE ENTIRE WORLD TO BELIEVE—PRAY!

"That they all may be one; as thou, Father, art in me, and I in thee, that they also may be one in us: that the world may believe that thou hast sent me." But the world is not believing our message that God sent Jesus. Why? Because we're not one. The world is watching us, and they want nothing to do with some Christians because we're not one. I predict to you this day that we will never be one and that the world will never believe until we come to a spiritual understanding of the power and significance of prayer. The process begins with the proclamation and moves to prayer. If you want to develop oneness that will be the envy of the world—pray! If you want to develop oneness that will cause the entire world to believe—pray! Pray that we may be one!

Back to Basics

Instead of setting aside time to pray, we set aside prayer. Too many of our churches are attempting to put prayer in context instead of creating a context for prayer. When we put prayer in context, we fit or force it between everything else. However, when we *create* a context for prayer, we make prayer the focus and fit everything else around it. We have to get back to basics. It is time for us to stop putting prayer in context and to start creating a context for prayer.

After all of their success, the newly developed church found itself at a crossroads—to continue business as usual or re-focus. The leaders chose to re-focus and re-proclaim prayer. Too often we get distracted and neglect to continue with what produces success. In the case of the early church, it was prayer. Our lack of stick-to-itiveness is a societal problem. We want to upgrade every time the technology changes, and we change whenever the fashion trends change. Fortunately, prayer is not updateable; there's no 2.0. Prayer is what it is! The only operating system that doesn't need an update is God's system. There are no "bugs" in His system. Consequently, there is no need for any type of updates. Likewise, prayer cannot be a fad; we don't do it simply because it's trending. God never intended it to be that way. He said pray always; pray without ceasing (Luke 21:36 and 1 Thessalonians 5:17).

Success in prayer cannot be taken for granted. When we treat prayer as a fad, we forfeit the power God intended us to have. As a result, we become a powerless group of people—one drawn by and to the next holy hype. When we encounter something of purported spiritual value, we treat it like a fad. We get what we can out of it while it is popular (trending), and we're ready to move to the next perceived best thing. In other words, we get involved in ministries in which we should not be involved because everyone else is doing it. We continually place our emphasis on the wrong things and in the wrong areas. Consequently, the wrong things and the wrong areas are becoming our focus while Christ is pushed aside. Yes, we're worshiping and praying, but we're praying for the wrong things and worshiping with the wrong motives (James 4:3).

Similarly, our attention span is so short that preachers and spiritual leaders are always looking for the next religious craze. If they don't provide what we think we should have, we're off to the next church because the current situation is not progressive enough. Consequently, some of our preachers, teachers, and leaders are becoming spiritual pop culture and fad pushers. If their sermons don't include references to the latest happenings and trending idioms, they feel that they're not reaching us, and we feel like we're not being fed.

WHAT WE DO IN WORSHIP NOW IS PRACTICE FOR
WHEN WE GET TO HEAVEN.

Proclaiming your church to be a house of prayer, and praying it into existence is hard work. Most of us, however, don't want to do the hard work. Spiritual leaders are seeking for success, but they're going about it the wrong way. They fail to realize that private prayer is what will lead to public success. Likewise, members come to church to be entertained. We behave as if we've purchased a ticket, and we sit back and wait for the talent show to begin. What's the saying? "Sit back, relax, and enjoy the show!"

The Bible says, "all flesh will come to worship him" (Isaiah 66:23). As such, we need to realize that what we do in our churches from week to week is practice—a rehearsal, if you please—for when we get to heaven. If our focus in worship is us now and it continues to be, we'll find it hard to redirect our worship to Him when we get to heaven. If we get to heaven!

What is even worse is that some of our spiritual leaders, who are chasing success, have become producers and directors of the weekly shows. Members are coming to be entertained, and they aim not to disappoint. When the curtains are drawn on Sabbath mornings, everyone and everything (the choir, band, and preachers) must be on point. Unfortunately, however, none of the performances point to Christ and prayer. It's almost as if the master plan is to make the churchgoer feel as if he is *not* in church when he is at church. This entire scenario is very puzzling and perplexing on so many levels.

Many of our churches, like the early church, began with Pentecostal power that roared through our communities with immense influence, changing lives. When we reflect on our successes, we're unable to point to anything else but the early mornings and late nights spent in prayer. In this postmodern era, however, prayer is passé. Hence, the Word of God is inert, the number of disciples is steadily declining, our spiritual leaders are faithless, and we're powerless to do wonders and miracles. Where necessary, we need to proclaim or re-proclaim the message that this house will be a house of prayer.

IN THIS POSTMODERN ERA, PRAYER IS PASSÉ.

When we look at Acts 6, we find the spiritual leaders of the new church poised to re-focus and re-proclaim prayer. They avoided becoming distracted by their success or the faddish wishes of the membership. They knew the source of their power and successive accomplishment. Hence, they said, "Halt everything, back to basics." "…we will give ourselves continually to prayer and to the ministry of the word" (Acts 6:4, KJV). Sometimes you have to go back to move forward. Again, look at what happened when they *re*-proclaimed prayer. The Word of God increased, the number of the disciples multiplied greatly, the priests were obedient to the faith, and Stephen did great wonders and miracles (Acts 6: 7, 8).

Ask yourself: have I proclaimed my church to be a house of prayer? If you have not, you must go back. If the answer is yes, you're ready to move forward.

Reflections

Notes

[1] Bounds, p. 186.

[2] Marshall B. Clinard and Robert F. Meier, *Sociology of Deviant Behavior* (15th ed.; Boston: Cengage Learning, 2016), p. 93.

[3] Charles H. Spurgeon, "The Power of Praying Together," *The Contemporaries Meet the Classics on Prayer*, ed. Leonard Allen (West Monroe, La.: Howard Publishing Company, 2003), p. 263.

[4] White, *Acts of the Apostles*, p. 549.

[5] *http://biblehub.com/commentaries/mhc/acts/1.htm.*

FOUR

Fruitful Ministries

*The blind and the lame came to him
at the temple, and he healed them.*

—Matthew 21:14 (NIV)

If you've proclaimed your church to be a house of prayer, then you're ready to begin the process of developing and implementing fruitful ministries (programs and activities) to meet the spiritual, physical, emotional, and social needs of your church and community. This is the *fourth* phase (see Figure 6) in becoming a house of prayer. By *prayerfully* removing spiritual robbers and proclaiming your church to be a house of prayer, you will create room for those in need.

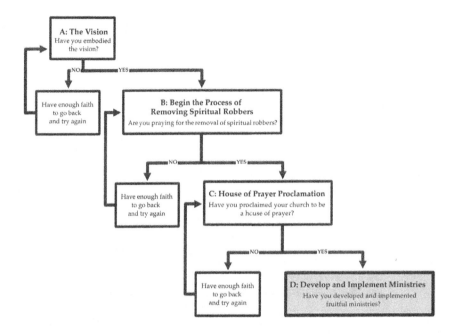

Figure 6.   Fruitful Ministries

Room Enough for Healing

Whenever you *prayerfully* drive out spiritual robbers and proclaim your church to be a house of prayer, you will have room enough in your church for those who stand in need of healing. But you also have to be alert. Whenever a void is created, it will be filled. If you *prayerfully* drive out spiritual robbers and don't intentionally put someone or something meaningful in place, anyone or anything will fill the resulting gap. Alas, it may not be who or what you want to fill the void. Therefore, you have to be ready to meet those in need of healing by developing and implementing fruitful ministries.

If you don't create room by driving out spiritual robbers who are hanging out in God's house, your church may never become a house of prayer, and you may never have room to meet the needs of the church and community. As our churches continue to develop and grow in all things related to prayer, some of us may not be around to witness it. I know it's hard to envision since we've always been there, but individuals who refuse to line-up with God will be cut off. Why? God may remove them to create room for those who need healing.

The void created by *prayerfully* driving, throwing, or chasing out spiritual robbers (individuals, practices, and/or things that are preventing your church from becoming a house of prayer) will be filled by individuals in need of spiritual, physical, emotional, and social healing. Remember, whenever you create a void, someone or something will fill it. "The blind and the lame came to him at the temple, and he healed them" (Matthew 21:14, NIV). The unfortunate reality for most of our churches is this: the void is created, and then we're not ready to provide healing. In other words, we do nothing meaningful to fill the void.

I'm amazed at the swiftness with which the temple filled-up again after Jesus cleared it. Note, there were no evangelistic meetings, no crusades, no revivals, no literature distribution, no conferences, no promotions, and no radio or church bulletin announcements. After Jesus made the proclamation, in the very next verse, it says, "The blind and the lame came to him at the temple, and he healed them" (Matthew 21:14, KJV).

That verse sounds to me like the blind and the lame had to have been in close proximity to the temple, simply waiting to get in. In other words, they wanted to be at church and they needed to be at church, but they were prevented from doing so because of the spiritual robbers. The blind and the lame could not get in because commerce had replaced prayer and healing. They were waiting to get in but were unable to do so because individuals with their own agendas were using the church for their personal gain.

...And They Will Come

Moreover, notice that Jesus did not go to them; they came to Him. When the first opportunity presented itself, the lame and the blind came to Him in the temple. Similarly, when we allow our churches to become houses of prayer, we'll be amazed at how individuals will line up to get in. Still, we must be ready to respond. The people came because of their personal need for spiritual, physical, emotional, and social healing.

What was happening in the temple was not meeting the needs of the community. Comparably, what is happening in some of our churches today is not meeting the needs of our communities. Like the individuals outside the temple in Jerusalem, our communities are looking for healing and will come seeking to be healed. You're saying to yourself, "No problem; we've got plenty of room." Physically, yes, our churches can handle the crowd, but spiritually, no. Neither you nor I can see the demonic forces that are at work taking up space and keeping individuals from being healed—all because we're not praying.

GET READY; THE BLIND AND THE LAME ARE COMING!

I said it earlier, and I'll say it again. Everyone in your church today will not be there next week, next month, or next year. Their long-term membership does not guarantee lifetime membership. As you continue to pray, know that your prayers will drive out spiritual robbers and overturn anyone and/or anything who is keeping your church from becoming a house of prayer.

Some of you are uncomfortable with what I'm saying; don't be. Just know that God will not allow me or anyone else to touch His people. You're safe and should feel at ease if you're doing what you know to be right. Furthermore, you should be comfortable with what has and will happen in your church because God is in control. Develop and implement fruitful ministries, and they will come. Get ready; the blind and the lame are coming!

Foundation, Walls, and Roof

A greater public good is achieved through prayer coupled with ministry than by any autonomous program or activity planned, developed, and implemented by a church. While the buying and selling of religious items to perform the then required sacrifices was a huge convenience to those attending services in the temple, Jesus knew that a greater public good would be accomplished if the temple were to become a place of prayer and not a mall or convenience store.

For most of us to ascertain and acknowledge that our legacy, convenience, and comfort is not Jesus' main priority is difficult. Know that He does care equally about our convenience and comfort as He does about our salvation. However, at times, He will displace our legacy, disrupt our convenience, and disturb our comfort to save us. Yet He will not risk our salvation to preserve that legacy, to ensure our convenience, or to make us comfortable.

Individuals in need of spiritual, physical, emotional, and social healing will come to your church. If you've prayerfully developed and implemented fruitful ministries, you'll be able to meet their needs. A house of prayer is always able to meet the needs of all. However, without prayer, a church will only satisfy the needs of a few. You will have minimal-to-no success in ministry without prayer. Know that "nothing is done well without prayer for the simple reason that it leaves God out of the work."[1]

Your ministries must be established on (foundation), surrounded by (walls), and covered by (roof) prayer. When you make your church a house of prayer by instituting prayer as the foundation, walls and roof, you will be in one accord, and the latter rain will fall. Subsequently, all ministries that you prayerfully plan, develop, and implement will be successful...

- But not successful in that the church has standing room only on most Sabbaths, or that you have three worship services.

- But not successful in that you're on television or that your tithes and offerings have doubled.

The success to which I am referring is that someone got to the throne of grace. *Take my people higher!*

Quantity is not an indication of success or of God's blessing. Regarding God and spiritual matters, it's not about volume or size but about the spiritual substance and spiritual impact of your activities. As such, I would rather be associated with a church of 40 praying members with the capacity for 400 than to be with a church at capacity without praying members. What a sad commentary on the life of our churches that we failed to lead anyone to Christ because we neglected to obey His Word! The life, power, and glory of our churches is prayer. Prayer is it!

QUANTITY IS NOT AN INDICATION OF SUCCESS
OR OF GOD'S BLESSING.

We must be ever vigilant because "the enemy never ceases in his endeavor to keep us from praying, for he knows that if a work is not founded on a great prayer effort, it lacks the power to stand in times of attack and shaking."[2] Reflecting this point of view, Dan Kelly, commenting on a Christian Spirituality Seminar conducted by Dr. Joseph Kiddler, notes that church growth is not so much a matter of programs and plans as it is prayer and preparation.[3] Accordingly, "if prayer does not inspire, sanctify, and direct our work, then self-will enters and ruins both the work and worker."[4]

In giving instructions about worship, Paul was very clear in what must happen first. He said: "The first thing I want you to do is pray" (1 Timothy 2:1, MSG). Prayer is the foundation, it is the walls, and it is the roof. Prayer is the thread that binds every person, every worship experience, and every ministry together. How foolish it would be for us to plan, develop, and implement any ministry without prayer—on what foundation, on whose authority, under what covering? If God would pull back the veil, we would be amazed at how prayer mingled with ministries has saved many souls. It is not the ministry; it is prayer.

No prayer, no unity!
No unity, no power!
No power, no healing!
No healing, no salvation!

Core Values

History has shown that successful organizations do an excellent job at helping their associates understand and embody the core values of the organization. If they are able to do this successfully, customers are happy, employees are engaged, and the organization develops a good reputation. As a result, whatever their product or service, it becomes the product or service of choice. Similarly, they also become an employer of choice. Placing a list of these core values in the employee's handbook, on nice posters throughout the building, or on the organization's website is not enough.

I would venture to say that most organizations have core values. They may not know it, but they do. A list of values is in place that drives the organization. Sadly, however, for some organizations, the values remain in someone's head, on his desk, or in a committee; they are never implemented. Successful organizations do their best to weave their core values into everything they do—from the day the new employee is on board to the yearly performance review and everything in between. Successful organizations do whatever is necessary to help their associates understand, embrace, embody, and live out their core values.

WHAT YOU PUT IN IS WHAT YOU GET OUT
— INPUT EQUALS OUTPUT.

Two indispensable core values of any Christian church must be a relationship with Christ and prayer. Core values that are understood, embraced, embodied, and lived out among members will have a tremendous impact on their ability to engage in successful ministry. What you put in is what you get out—input equals output. The fundamental point about the association between core values (a relationship with Christ and prayer) and a church's ability to provide fruitful ministries, is a point which most spiritual leaders miss.

We currently live in a society where individuals are more moved by events than by relationships. Too often we attend church or participate in spiritual activities associated with certain events—Easter, Christmas, New Year's, etc. If we were moved by our relationship with Christ, we would be more committed to Him and ministry. Too many of our churches are focused on the event and are not helping members to develop a relationship with Christ through prayer. When we are event-oriented instead of relationship-oriented, it becomes that much harder to engage members in fruitful ministry.

A relationship with Christ and prayer, coupled with hardworking members, will render your ministries successful. Herein lies the problem: our spiritual leaders are not doing a good job at helping their members to understand and embody the core values of a relationship with Christ and prayer. Giving these core values lip service is not enough; it must be woven into everything the church does. Most of our churches connect spiritually with members in such a superficial manner, it's no wonder they only get surface commitment and service in return. Again, inputs equal outputs.

The personal "do-it-for-me" appeal to engage members in ministry (absent a spiritual connection through the core values of a relationship with Christ and prayer), unfortunately, will only get us so far. On the other hand, if we're able to connect spiritually with a member, we can get him/her to do anything. Why? They're committed and moved to serve because they are doing it for Christ—not you. When this happens, members are engaged for service, the community is happy, and the church develops a good reputation. When we engage members at this fundamental level, churches will be successful in meeting the spiritual, physical, emotional, and social needs of their communities. Subsequently, the church will become the church of choice.

Prayerless Ministries

The Devil is a master psychologist; he understands our self-centeredness and feeds it at the expense of prayer and subsequent spiritual growth. Due to our borderline narcissistic personality, he's able to get us preoccupied with so many different ministries that are more about making us feel good about ourselves than they are about actually meeting the needs of the church and community. Don't get me wrong; there is great social and spiritual value in feeding and clothing the homeless, visiting the sick, passing out literature, tutoring children, visiting those in prison, etc. Too often, however, we get caught up in filling up the stat sheet.

Ministry after ministry gets started while the spiritual lives of the church and the surrounding community remains unchanged. Unfortunately, we never pause to prayerfully conduct the investigation into the spiritual value of the ministry. We hear the passionate appeals, become emotionally moved, and charge forward under the misguided impression that we're doing something good. Nevertheless, our involvement only satisfies our self-centeredness. Yes, we're doing good, but it comes at a spiritual cost. What we don't realize is that the Devil—the master psychologist—is at work to keep us busy with non-fruit producing, feel-good ministries all to achieve his master plan of keeping us prayerless.

"As activity increases and men become successful in doing any work for God, there is a danger of trusting to human plans and methods. There is a tendency to pray less and to have less faith."[5] No ministry will succeed without prayer. You cannot start a ministry where prayer is nowhere to be found. We must take our example from Jesus. What did Jesus do before He began the various stages of His ministry? He prayed. Why do we think we can do otherwise?

I want you to understand that God can and will bless and use the ministries that you start, but somewhere, somebody has to pray and continue to pray. What happens is that we begin the process, we get going, the ministry is up and running, but we've never prayed about it. For some others, we stop praying. This is when Satan comes right in. You have to start with prayer and keep praying.

For example, if you start a marriage club and the focus becomes relational and sexual health and not prayer, the club will fail. Though it may appear to be successful, the club will not bear much fruit. Moreover, we could plan and execute the best worship services by having a high time every Sabbath, but without prayer no one will mature spiritually. We'll have a form of godliness without any power. If you're planning and implementing all forms of ministries and you're not praying, the Devil is exceedingly jubilant.

Beyond being a place where God meets with us (Exodus 25:8), what is the real point of the church? What value does a church add to our community? We could worship anywhere, but God designed a plan whereby we would set up a literal, visual outpost, where those in need can find retreat, refuge, and restoration. Such rejuvenation, however, can only come through prayer and fruitful ministries.

IF YOU'RE NOT PRAYING, EVERY MINISTRY WILL

EVENTUALLY FAIL, FOLD, OR FALL.

Too many individuals in our churches and in our communities are wandering around uninspired and unsaved because we're too busy administrating, preaching, and singing; but not praying. Sometimes the distractions from prayer can occur right in church. Occasionally, the distractions from prayer can be the worship experience itself. Presently our churches are known for everything else but prayer. We're famous for our programs and activities, but not for being houses of prayer. If you're not praying, you don't have the power that is necessary to be a conduit for healing—for yourself or anyone else. If you're not praying, every ministry will eventually fail, fold, or fall.

The following quotes unequivocally describe our state of prayer-lessness as a church—to the great delight of Satan:

> E. M. Bounds points out that "prayer is absolutely necessary if we want to carry on God's work properly. Sacred work or church activities may make us so busy that they hinder praying; and when this is the case, evil always results."[6]

> Dennis Smith notes, "Satan wants to confuse the believer concerning prayer. He wants to keep us from understanding the vital role prayer plays in the work of God in this earth and in saving the lost. Satan knows that if he can get the Christian to be negligent in the area of prayer, he has little to fear concerning the believer's spiritual growth in Christ or his effectiveness as a laborer for God in His work on earth. Satan is more afraid of the praying Christian than the active, working Christian, which is why he will do all in his power to keep you from becoming a Spirit-filled, Spirit-directed prayer intercessor for God."[7]

> Samuel Chadwick asserts, "Satan dreads nothing but prayer. The church that lost its Christ was full of good works. Activities are multiplied that meditation may be ousted, and organizations are increased that prayer may have no chance. Souls may be lost in good works, as surely as in evil ways. The one concern of the Devil is to keep the saints from praying. He fears nothing from prayerless studies, prayerless work, prayerless religion. He laughs at our toil, mocks at our wisdom, but trembles when we pray."[8]

> Similarly, R. A. Torrey states, "the great cry of our day is work, work, work, new organizations, new methods,

new machinery; the great need of our day is prayer. It was a masterstroke of the Devil when he got the church so generally to lay aside this mighty weapon of prayer. The Devil is perfectly willing that the church should multiply its organizations and deftly contrive machinery for the conquest of the world for Christ if it will only give up praying. He laughs as he looks at the church today and says to himself: you can have your Sunday schools and your young people's societies, your Young Men's Christian Associations and your Women's Christian Temperance Unions, your Boys' Brigades, your grand choirs and your fine organs, your brilliant preachers and your revival efforts too, if you don't bring the power of Almighty God into them by earnest, persistent, believing, mighty prayer."[9]

Charles Stanley observes the same. He notes, "Satan is not concerned with how many times we go to church or how many hymns we sing. He does not feel threatened by our organizations or cutting-edge technologies. But when God's people fall on their knees and claim Christ's power and authority, everything in heaven will begin to move, and everything in hell will begin to shake."[10]

Fruit Bearing

The process of fruit production is not a one or two-week process. Fruit bearing is a lengthy and prayerful process before a harvest is realized. If you and/or your church, as a whole, have developed ministries, you should be able to ask and honestly answer this question: have I developed and implemented fruitful ministries? I use the word "fruitful," because *fruitful* means that the ministry is bearing something of spiritual value. In other words, individuals are being healed spiritually, physically, emotionally, and/or socially.

Too often we dream up "grow-bigger-quick" schemes, forgetting that fruit production is a process. We dream up ministries that are deficient in spiritual sensibility; the potential for fruit bearing is greatly lacking. An idea for ministry is just that, an idea, until you blend it with prayer. At that point, it becomes a spiritual idea—one that God would bless and assist you in implementing if He gets the glory. "Success has nothing to do with how gifted or how resourced you are; it has everything to do with glorifying God in any and every situation by making the most of it."[11]

Herein lies the problem. We dream up these ministries for our personal gain and glory. Our spiritual minds are so twisted that we've squeezed God out of His rightful place in our lives and churches. What we fail to realize is that when the ministry bears fruit and God gets the glory, by default, some of the glory will fall on us. His glory is so wide and so bright that it will not miss you (Exodus 33:18-23; 34:29-35). We must prayerfully consider the ministries we implement to ensure that God gets His glory. God does not mind sharing, but it has to be His choice.

"Ministries are seriously deluded when they think they are prospering and yet do not see any conversions."[12] If you've started a ministry that is not bearing anything, you need to stop it. Stop and prayerfully review the ministry, asking God what He would have you do. If you do this inventory, I assure you that He will bless you beyond the current level. Your ministry will grow and be exponentially fruitful. Too often we settle for scarcely fruitful or totally fruitless when God wants to bless us exponentially. Why do we settle for a few souls when God is willing and able to supply thousands daily?

I'm often disappointed when churches don't realize it, but their actions related to certain ministries signals to everyone, once again, that they're satisfied with mediocrity. Worse yet, their actions signal to God that they have no intention of giving Him their best. Accordingly, I don't believe that He will bless their efforts. God has or is withdrawing His blessings as we continue to give Him "less than" and think that we're giving Him our best. We're doing it across the board (worship, ministry, business, evangelism), and God is not pleased. Remember, spiritual robbers are not only individuals but can also be practices and things. For example, a church having to deal with the lack of finances distracts from moving God's church forward. Most times, we can't even focus on financially supporting "genuine" ministries because we're too absorbed with managing futile ministries. God help us!

We will not be able to provide healing to our churches and communities until we drive out spiritual robbers, proclaim our church to be a house of prayer, tap into the available power, and be ready to meet those in need of healing by developing and implementing fruitful ministries.

- If we don't *prayerfully* drive out the individuals, practices, and/or things that are preventing us from becoming a house of prayer—no healing.
- If we don't become a house of prayer—no fruit.
- If we don't get on the same page spiritually (one accord)—no healing.
- If we don't tap into His awesome power—no fruit.
- If we're not ready when the void is created—no healing.
- If we don't implement fruitful ministries—no fruit.

My overall concern is not so much the number of or types of ministries; I'm more so concerned that we're pursuing, starting, and continuing fruitless ministries. Because we're not praying, we have no evidence as to whether God wants us to pursue, start, or continue the ministry. Any ministry lacking that substantiation will be fruitless. Regrettably, we sometimes engage in and maintain ministries because they are someone's pet project. I have no issue with pet projects; we all have them. The question remains: is this the ministry that God would have you pursue? Is this the ministry that will lead another soul to Christ? If you're fully convinced, then prayerfully continue. If not, ask Him to clearly reveal the ministry in which He would have you involved.

As a church, we cannot afford to have ministries that are not providing healing and producing saints. Ministries are fruitless for three primary reasons. First, we begin the wrong ministry. Second, when we prayerfully identify the correct ministry, no one continues to pray. Third, we're working hard and not smart. Too many of us are working hard for Christ, but we're not working smart. The critical difference between hard and smart work is prayer. We're often able to get things done, but we can get so much more done for Christ if we include prayer. When we begin the ministry with prayer and pray through it, our efforts become smart work.

WE CANNOT AFFORD TO HAVE MINISTRIES THAT ARE NOT PROVIDING HEALING AND PRODUCING SAINTS.

Some churches and/or individuals plant pine trees with the misguided assumption that they'll produce pineapples because the word *pine* is in the name. If the ministry is not fruitful, stop it and prayerfully start over. Ask yourself: have I developed and implemented fruitful ministries (programs and activities) to meet the needs of my church and community? If you have not, you must go back and try again. If the answer is yes, get ready to face attacks and distractions.

Reflections

Notes

1   Bounds, p. 528.

2   Sue Curran, *The Praying Church: Principles and Power of Corporate Praying* (Lake Mary, Fla.: Creation House Press, 2001), p. 20.

3   Dan L. Kelly, "Church Learns Simple Method for Church Growth," *The Atlantic Union Gleaner* (February 2007), p. 18.

4   Bounds, p. 164.

5   Ellen G. White, *Desire of Ages* (Boise Ida.: Pacific Press Publishing Association, 1940), p. 362.

6   Bounds, p. 527.

7   Dennis Smith, *Spirit Baptism and Prayer* (*www.spiritbaptism.org, 2008*), pp. 8, 12.

8   Samuel Chadwick (source unknown).

9   R. A. Torrey, *How to Pray* (Chicago: Moody Publishers, 2007), p. 119.

10 Charles Stanley, *Handle With Prayer: Unwrap the Source of God's Strength for Living* (Colorado Springs: David C. Cook, 2011), p. 29.

11 Batterson, p. 31.

12 Charles Spurgeon, *Spurgeon on Prayer and Spiritual Warfare* (New Kensington, Penn.: Whitaker House, 1998), p. 331.

FIVE

Attacks and Distractions

But when the chief priests and the teachers of the law
saw the wonderful things he did...
they were indignant.

—MATTHEW 21:15 (NIV)

I
f I were writing a movie script, at this point I would insert a note here to run the epilogue, which would read (while soft music played) as follows: "The Christian church became a house of prayer. Today, the Christian church is still growing as it continues to bear fruit for the kingdom." It would seem logical for the process of becoming a house of prayer to end with the development and implementation of fruitful ministries. Oh, how I wish it were so; regrettably it does not. Simply because we're trying to do as God wants does not mean we'll be immune to problems, frustrations, and attacks.[1] Quite the opposite is actually true. If you've developed and implemented

fruitful ministries, be prepared for attacks and distractions. This is the *fifth* phase (see Figure 7) in the process of becoming a house of prayer. Understand that Satan will not sit idly by and allow your church to become a fruit-bearing house of prayer. Consequently, you and your church must be prepared for attacks and distractions. Satan will become infuriated and will unleash a massive assault.

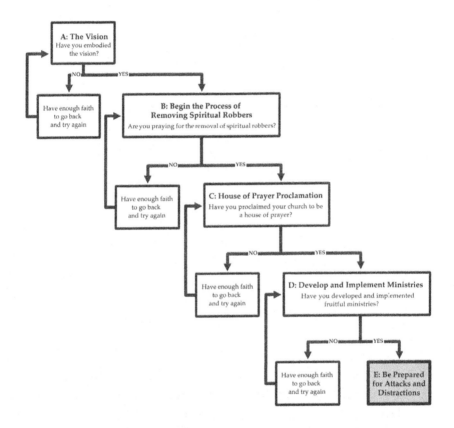

Figure 7. Attacks and Distractions

Spiritual Murder

Have you noticed that whenever God is about to promote you, elevating you to a larger sphere of service or a higher platform of spiritual life, that you always get thrown down?[2] If you don't believe me, take a look at Mark and Luke's accounts of this incident. "The chief priests and the teachers of the law heard this and began looking for a way to kill him…" (Mark 11:18). "Every day He was teaching at the temple. But the chief priests, the teachers of the law and the leaders among the people were trying to kill him" (Luke 19:47). When the chief priests, teachers, and leaders saw Jesus' driving out the robbers, heard His proclamation, and saw that He had developed and implemented fruitful ministries, they wanted to kill Him. The same could happen to you.

Who were these haters? Who were the chief priests, teachers, and leaders? While it's Biblical, I'm embarrassed to say it, but the chief priests, teachers, and leaders were the religious leaders. Sometimes the attacks and distractions will come from your own spiritual leaders. When the spiritual leaders saw that the implemented ministries were bearing fruit and that individuals were being healed spiritually, physically, emotionally, and socially, they became fearful, displeased, jealous, angry, indignant, and wanted to kill Christ.

The human view of life that expects nothing but sunshine and looks merely for ease, pleasure, and flowers is an entirely false view of life and shows supreme ignorance.[3] If you have a strong desire for God's name, kingdom, and will, your troubles will automatically become great.[4] No matter how wonderfully the Lord has worked on your behalf, spiritual enemies are still arrayed against you, and their spiritual attacks must be faced until Jesus comes again.[5] Accordingly, "when you get zealous for God, nobody will hate you more than the Christian who has no fervency for Jesus."[6]

SOMETIMES THE ATTACKS AND DISTRACTIONS
WILL COME FROM YOUR OWN SPIRITUAL LEADERS.

You are under attack; we are under attack. And the worst attacks sometimes are from within, which is why leaders and members who stand for what is right often stand alone. Whenever you venture to do great things for Christ, Satan will assail you. Jesus knew this, and through Paul, He provided clear instructions in Ephesians 6:11-18. We're told to put on the whole armor of God that we may be able to stand against the wiles of the Devil. Specifically, stand with your loins girded, put on your breastplate, and shod your feet. Above all, take your shield, helmet, and sword. Then He ends by saying to pray always. Why would we get these instructions if He did not expect us to deal with shenanigans? Why would God tell us to put on such armor if He did not expect us to be involved in battle?

It will happen. Whenever you develop and implement fruitful ministries for Christ and when the ministries begin to bear fruit, you will face attacks and distractions. God is blessing, and Satan is not happy. Individuals in the community, family members, church members, and/or spiritual leaders will begin to fear you. They will become so jealous and angry that they will want to kill you. It may not be physical, but they will attempt spiritual murder. While they may not be bold enough to risk a prison sentence under our current judicial system, they're bold enough to risk their soul's salvation to commit spiritual murder. Very interesting! These individuals will allow themselves to be used by the Devil to kill spiritual progress. It will happen. Why? How? Allow me to illustrate why and how it will happen.

Killing Giants

Jim Cymbala notes that "…when a new ministry for Christ begins or when someone steps out in faith to do God's will, Satan will often try to squelch what God is doing right at the outset—before it gathers momentum and builds a stronger faith."[7] He continues, "Whenever people stir themselves to seek the Lord, whenever someone steps out in faith upon God's promises, whenever a fresh consecration is made to yield oneself completely to him—that is the very time when Satan's most cunning attacks will often occur."[8] You're going to be attacked and distracted. Why? To answer that question, we must ask another question: when is the best time to kill a giant?[9]

The best time to kill a giant is as a baby. Giants are not born as giants in excess of seven, eight, nine, or ten feet tall. Had David encountered Goliath as a baby or even as a five-year-old boy, the extraordinary narrative of conquest found in 1 Samuel 17 would have been considerably less remarkable. The answer is an astonishingly obvious one, yet too often we allow the assassin to strike without any resistance.

If someone were attacking you and you had a weapon, in all likelihood you would use it. Well, the Devil is attacking us, and prayer is a weapon, but we don't use it. We've become so incapacitated with our superficial success (preaching, large churches, television shows, Facebook likes) and have holstered our weapon of prayer. As a result, the giant that God intended us to be by coupling true prayer with preaching, for example, never becomes a reality.

PRAYER IS A WEAPON, AND WE DON'T USE IT.

Too many of us allow infants of greed, selfishness, hatred, and all manner of vice to grow in our lives until they become giants. We allow them to grow until they become uncontrollable, defiant, taunting giants—making us dismayed and greatly afraid (1 Samuel 17:11, KJV). These giants, once infants, taunt us like Goliath taunted the Israelites—morning and evening (1 Samuel 17:16). With this, Satan has no problem. Conversely, he will not allow babes of true love, earnest prayer, and genuine worship to become giants in our lives. He will do his best to snuff them out before they can become giants. As I have already asserted, the best time to kill a would-be giant is as a baby.

How? The scripture contains a few examples of would-be giants who Satan attempted to assassinate at an early age. Respectively, Joseph, Moses, and Jesus were supposed to move God's people to a higher level physically (provide food), socially (provide freedom), and spiritually (provide salvation). Satan's plan, however, was to take them out before they could implement God's agenda.

For example, God had special plans for Joseph. He had designated Joseph to ascend to positions of great authority. In said positions, he would be the supplier of food who would rescue not only his family but also an entire nation from starvation. However, at an early age Joseph's brothers developed envy and hatred for him and attempted to kill him.

Similarly, God had selected Moses for a great task. His mission was to redeem Israel from slavery. Moses was chosen by God to be a leader, a deliverer. He was to lead God's people out of Egypt and into the Promised Land. However, as a baby, his life was in danger when Pharaoh gave orders to throw all newborn boys into the Nile. Knowing his charge, the Devil attempted to take Moses out before he became a man.

Like Joseph and Moses, God had preordained a path to greatness for Jesus. His assignment before the world began was to save mankind from sin. Jesus was chosen by God to be a leader, a redeemer. Orders were sent, however, to Bethlehem and the whole area that all the boys two years old and under were to be killed. Again, the Devil is not in the business of allowing would-be giants the opportunity to mature. The best time to kill a giant is as a baby.

Your Undoing

The best time to kill prayer is before it begins to bear fruit. When the Devil perceives that your church is beginning to bear fruit and when he observes that your church as a baby will become a giant, he will attack and distract you. The best time to prevent a house of prayer from becoming a house of prayer is at the start. However, if Satan is unable to kill a giant at birth, he will continue to seek every opportunity to kill it as an adult before it becomes even more powerful.

Satan was unsuccessful in killing Jesus at birth. That failure, however, did not prevent future attempts on his life until Satan thought he was successful some thirty years later. Likewise, the same will happen in your church. You'll get to six months or a year of praying, and you'll develop a false sense of accomplishment. You'll assume that all will be fine; after all, you've been praying. Know, however, that the attempts to destroy prayer will continue relentlessly until the Devil and his associates surmise that they've won.

THE BEST TIME TO KILL PRAYER
IS BEFORE IT BEGINS TO BEAR FRUIT.

Concern for God's house will be your undoing (John 2:17, TLB). When you attempt to hold God's standards, His requests of you, and His commands high in your church, it will be the catalyst for your undoing. You will suffer attacks and distractions by individuals in the community, family members, church members, and by spiritual leaders of your church. These individuals knowingly or unknowingly are allowing themselves to be used by the Devil. While the attacks and distractions will be personal, don't take it personally. The Devil's aim is not you; you're just in his way. Your undoing is collateral damage; his aim—his target—is prayer.

"The ultimate measure of a man is not where he stands in moments of comfort and convenience, but where he stands at times of challenge and controversy."[10] Where are you standing? Know without question that "the Father never allows difficulty just for the sake of difficulty—there is always a higher purpose."[11] As a believer in the power of prayer, you can't hold it against your attackers and distractors. There is a greater force at work that can only be checked by your prayers.

Attacks and distractions will come as you engage your church in the process of becoming a house of prayer. Oh, how I wish it were not so, but regrettably it is. Know, however, that the Lord has sworn to fight your battles. He states unequivocally: "I will fight against whoever fights you" (Isaiah 49:25, GNT). While Satan's attacks will not overcome you or your church (God's will, will be done), you must be prepared to walk away praying, knowing that you've done your best.

Reflections

Notes

1   Dave Earley, *The 21 Most Effective Prayers of the Bible* (Uhrichsville, Ohio: Barbour Publishing, 2005), p. 103.

2   Spurgeon, *Spurgeon on Prayer and Spiritual Warfare*, p. 109.

3   Bounds, p. 313.

4   Watchman Nee, *The Prayer Ministry of the Church* (New York: Christian Fellowship Publishers, 1973), p. 54.

5   Jim Cymbala, *The Church God Blesses* (Grand Rapids: Zondervan, 2002), p. 100.

6   Sorge, p. 163.

7   Cymbala, p. 13.

8   Ibid, p. 31.

9   Dexter Ravenell, Personal Communication.

10 Martin Luther King, Jr., *Strength to Love* (New York: Harper & Row Publishers, 1963), p. 25.

11 Stanley, p. 10.

SIX

Walk Away Praying

*And He left them and went out of the city
to Bethany, where He spent the night.*

—MATTHEW 21:17 (NIV)

As far as I am concerned, God turned into good what you meant for evil, for he brought me to this high position I have today so that I could save the lives of many people" (Genesis 50:20, TLB). This profound statement by Joseph is assurance that God was in control of his situation and is still in control of our situation. The high position to which He has brought us is His throne of grace, and the saving of lives refers to soul salvation for others—co-laboring with God to finish His work. When you've been attacked and distracted from God's purpose for your life and His church, walking away is often difficult, but you may have to do it. Don't be shy about walking away while praying. The *sixth* phase (see Figure 8) in the process of becoming a house of prayer is knowing when to walk away praying.

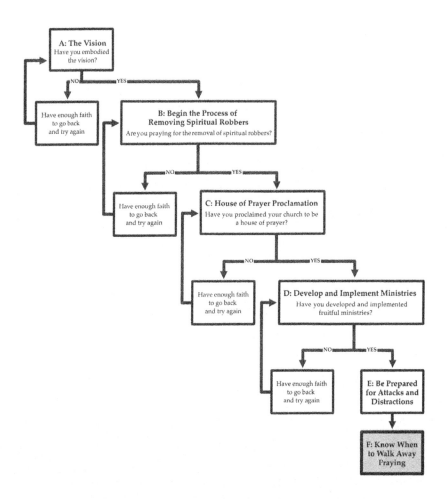

Figure 8. Walking Away

Know When

Compared to others, I would not consider myself a country music fan. Nevertheless, every so often there is a song that transcends its genre and becomes a crossover hit. "The Gambler," recorded by Kenny Rogers, is one such song. I can still recall hearing and singing the catchy refrain: "...know when to fold 'em, know when to walk away, and know when to run..."[1] "The Gambler," like many country songs, tells a story and has a message. On the contrary, I don't want you to fold; I don't want you to run, but you may have to walk away praying.

As humans, it's difficult for us to comprehend and acknowledge what is occurring in the spiritual realm. Prayer (communication with God) is the best way—no, the only way— for us to gain that understanding, and at some level, acquire an awareness of what is happening in the spiritual realm. In the spiritual realm, praying is a sign of your need for divine assistance and intervention. Praying is never a sign of weakness. Don't allow anyone to convince you otherwise. Praying actually puts you in a position of strength. By praying you move the battle out of the physical realm and into the spiritual. In the spiritual realm, victory is already guaranteed. While walking away (your season of spiritual retreat), know that praying moves you to a position of incomparable strength.

You have to know when to walk away, but you have to walk away praying. Though difficult to do, you'll have to do it. Again, taking this step is biblical; I'm not making it up. "And He left them and went out of the city to Bethany, where He spent the night" (Matthew 21:17, NIV). The verse reads, "He left them"; He walked away from the individuals in the community, including family members, church members, and spiritual leaders. "And when evening came, He went out of the city" (Mark 11:19, KJV). "He went out" is walking away. I don't know how else to interpret these statements. The question, however, remains: what do you do when you've done your best? Simple answer, difficult act: you walk away praying.

PRAYING IS NEVER A SIGN OF WEAKNESS.

Nights in Prayer

It's a simple answer and a difficult act; yet there is a deeper purpose. You're not simply walking away praying; you're retreating to refortify yourself. Why is there a need for refortification? Because the Devil is trying to wear you down and out (Daniel 7:25). When Jesus walked away, He did not walk away so that He could sleep. His retreat was not so much that He might sleep undisturbed, but that He might pray undisturbed. Jesus walked away so that He could pray. Herbert Lockyer notes, "…prayer was His regular habit and His resort in every emergency."[2] Whenever Jesus' ministry or mission was faced with a crisis, He spent the entire night in prayer.

For example, Luke 6:12 (KJV) says, "And it came to pass in those days, that he went out into a mountain to pray, and continued all night in prayer to God." It was another Sabbath, and Jesus was in the temple teaching and healing. In other words, He was involved in fruitful ministry. Remember, whenever your ministry begins to bear fruit, it will face attacks and distractions. Likewise, the spiritual leaders were seeking an opportunity to accuse Jesus. Hence, they called a church executive council meeting to discuss a plan to destroy Him (Luke 6:6-11). What did Jesus do? He walked away praying. He found a quiet place, and He prayed all night.

The all-night prayer session on the night Jesus was betrayed is another example of how He spent the entire night in prayer when faced with a crisis (Matthew 26:36-46). In Gethsemane, Jesus was sorrowful and troubled. He had a full and clear vision of all the sufferings that were before Him. As a result, Jesus wanted to find a quiet place to pray because He knew what was to come—the cross. Like Jesus, when we're faced with a problem, we need to get off the phone, turn off the e-mail, stop texting, stop posting, and find a quiet place to pray. Stop telling everyone else and tell Jesus. Having faced difficulties and with future struggles ahead, all we can do is pray. Remember, retreating to pray is not folding or running; rather, it is an exercise in refortifying yourself.

STOP TELLING EVERYONE ELSE AND TELL JESUS.

Like Jesus, the disciples knew when to walk away praying. They had a good teacher, and they were good students. In Acts 4, the spiritual leaders are again on the attack. Peter and John were arrested and jailed because they were involved in fruitful ministry. Remember, whenever your ministry begins to bear fruit, it will face attacks and distractions. Threatened to discontinue their ministry and then released from jail, Peter and John found their friends, retreated, and prayed for greater boldness. Whenever we're faced with attacks and distractions, we must do the same. God answered the disciples' prayers, and the Holy Spirit filled them.

Right to Fight

It's a tough thing to do, but we must be willing to walk away and allow God to fight our battles. When you know that you've done your best in what God has called you to do, you can turn the other cheek to individuals in the community, family members, church members, and even spiritual leaders who have attacked and distracted you. In the Sermon on the Mount, Jesus made it clear that we are to walk away. He said, "Don't fight back against someone who wants to do harm to you. If they hit you on the right cheek, let them hit the other cheek too" (Matthew 5:39, ERV).

Similarly, Jesus imparted specific instructions to His apostles as He sent them out to witness (Matthew 10:5-42). He knew that everyone would not be receptive to His message, and thus, provided directives in dealing with individuals who did not accept them. He said, "...if they don't welcome you, quietly withdraw. Don't make a scene. Shrug your shoulders and be on your way" (Matthew 10:14, MSG).

The gospel of Mark puts it this way: "And whenever a village won't accept you or listen to you, shake off the dust from your feet as you leave; it is a sign that you have abandoned it [the village] to its fate" (Mark 6:11, TLB). In the same way, Jesus knew that we would have spiritual robbers who would reject His charge to us. His directives to us are the same—walk away (quietly withdraw). Don't make a scene; shake off the dust from your feet as you leave; walk away praying.

Satan had Jesus right where he wanted him, and he thought that he had finally defeated Him. Jesus, nevertheless, maintained His silence. What an awesome thought that our salvation resulted from a Savior who knew when to walk away! "He was oppressed and he was afflicted, yet he never said a word. He was brought as a lamb to the slaughter; and as a sheep before her shearers is dumb, so he stood silent before the ones condemning him" (Isaiah 53:7, TLB). He knew when to walk away by keeping silent. Note, however, that He did not simply walk away; He walked away praying. He said, "…Father, forgive them; for they know not what they do…" (Luke 23:34, KJV).

Some of us will have to do the same. When you're facing attacks and distractions, you'll have to remain silent and walk away praying the same prayer: "Father, forgive them; for they know not what they do." Knowing that you're right does not give you the right to fight. This concept, however, goes against all that our society teaches. Society says, "An eye for an eye! If you're right, stand up and defend yourself!" No! Being right does not give you the right to fight. We must learn to turn the other cheek, shake the dust off our feet, and maintain our silence. We must allow God to fight our battles. You have to know when to walk away, praying for the betterment of the whole.

Get Out of the Way

God's favor, His blessings, will often produce an equal in intensity and force, but an opposite reaction from the Devil. Whenever God is about to favor you and/or His church, Satan will try to sidetrack you. He knows that he cannot win, but the attacks and distractions are a way to buy additional time. But hold on; God's favor will reach its intended target. You may not be around to see it become a reality, but it will transpire. In praising John the Baptist, Jesus noted that the scriptures declared, "I'm sending my messenger on ahead to make the road smooth for you" (Luke 7:27, MSG). Understand that you may simply be a forerunner, and now it is time for you to get out of the way.

GOD IS NOT CONCERNED ABOUT OUR INDIVIDUAL ACCOMPLISHMENTS AND SELF-ACTUALIZATION.

Sometimes staying around has the potential to cause more harm than good. You know you're not toxic. I know you're not toxic. God knows you're not toxic. But you may be toxic to the current situation. Sometimes if you stay, you may cause a division in the church. Your presence may result in individuals' taking sides. Remember, God is not concerned about our individual accomplishments and self-actualization. He's trying to save souls. Do your best while the circumstances permit, but walk away praying if you must go. Walking away praying, when instructed, sets you up for a comeback—an opportunity to try again.

Reflections

_____

_____

_____

_____

_____

_____

_____

_____

_____

_____

_____

_____

_____

_____

Notes

1 Don Schlitz, *The Gambler,* Vinyl, United Artists, 1978.

2 Herbert Lockyer, *All the Prayers of the Bible* (Grand Rapids: Zondervan, 1959), p. 180.

SEVEN

Try Again

Early in the morning,
as He was on His way back to the city,
He was hungry.

—Matthew 21:18 (NIV)

Whom you've been attacked and distracted from God's purpose for your life and His church and you've been instructed to walk away, remember that you're walking away to retreat and refortify yourself through prayer. The perceptive understanding of the vision that God's house, your church, must become a house of prayer is one that you will never disregard. Encountering challenges while attempting to cast this vision is to be expected. Moreover, the struggles may become so acute that God may direct you to walk away. The vision, however, never dies, and you must have enough faith to try one more time. The *seventh* and final phase (see Figure 9) in the process of becoming a house of prayer is having enough faith to give it another try.

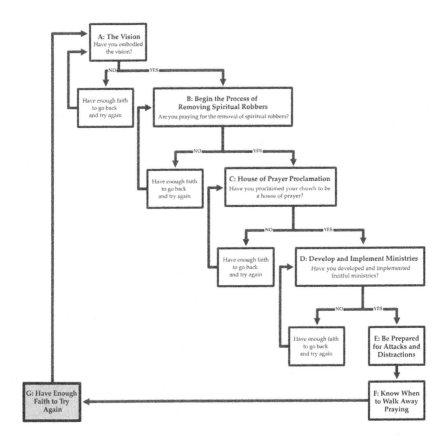

Figure 9. Try Again

Jim Cymbala points out that, "Opposition, jealousy and hatred should never cause us to become discouraged—driven off from our duty. Rather, these things should cause us to rejoice that God is up to something great."[1] The attacks and distractions will come. Again, bumping into challenges while attempting to cast the vision of prayer in your church is to be expected. In the spiritual realm, the linear progression of grief and distress is often more trouble, but then joy. Don't give up; don't give in. Know that "...weeping may endure for a night, but joy cometh in the morning" (Psalm 30:5, KJV).

Work to Be Done

Our focus text for this chapter reads: "Early in the morning, as He was on His way back to the city, He was hungry" (Matthew 21:18, NIV). Notice first that Jesus did not stay away. After being attacked and distracted, He did walk away to spend some time in prayer, but He did not stay away. Like Jesus, many of us will have to return to our churches and communities because there is still work to be done.

Where did He come back to? He came back to the same city. Some of us may be directed to another vineyard. Many of us, however, will have to return to the same church or community. We may have to return and labor again with the same church members and spiritual leaders who attacked and distracted us. Nevertheless, where and with whom, we must have enough faith to try again; there is much work to be done.

Notice also that Jesus returned to the city *early* in the morning. Many of us may be willing to go back to our church, community, or another vineyard, but only on our terms. God is saying to us the time of refortification is over; it is now time to go back. We, however, prefer to wait until we're ready. Too often we wait until late morning, the afternoon, or even until midnight, when we knew that we should have returned *early* in the morning. There is work to be done. Stop what you're doing, put aside your fears, and return to your church or community to recast the vision of prayer. If to another vineyard, go now! Go now, and cast the vision. Give it another try!

GOD IS SAYING TO US THE TIME OF
REFORTIFICATION IS OVER.

In Matthew 21:18 Jesus was described as being *hungry*. After your time away in prayer, you should return to your church and community hungry. If you're not, something is wrong. Are you hungry? So many of us are no longer hungry. Our urgency for the vision, for *prayerfully* expelling spiritual robbers, for proclaiming our church a house of prayer, and for developing and implementing fruitful ministries has waned. We've been so beat up and down by those attempting to prevent God's house from becoming a house of prayer that we've lost our appetite for souls.

Too many of us are returning to our churches and communities, but we're no longer hungry. Don't despair, however; I have good news. If you're hungry, I have a way for you to be nourished and filled. If it worked for Jesus, it will also work for you. Jesus said, "My nourishment comes from doing the will of God who sent me, and from finishing his work" (John 4:34, TLB). In the spiritual realm, your passion for souls—your hunger—can only be satisfied by doing what God has called you to do. His desire for us is that we return to our churches and communities to realize His will—finishing His work. Try again; there is work to be done.

Next, Try Victory

You don't know, but your next try casting the vision for prayer in your church could result in a house of prayer—victory! Because you have enough faith to give it one more chance, it will result in a *next-try* victory. You live in a state of expectancy, and you're not apprehensive to try again. Each night ends with the thought that tomorrow could be the day, and each day begins with the hope that today is the day. You don't know whether the victory will come with the second, seventh, or tenth try, but you'll have enough faith to try again. The following are a few examples of what I call a *next-try* victory.

a. In Exodus chapters 3-11, Moses was called, prepared, and used by God for his mission. "Go tell Pharaoh, 'Let My people go.'" Moses embodied the vision and went to Pharaoh, but he was rejected. God said to him, "Go back. Tell Pharaoh that he is not listening!" The result? Plague one: blood. Pharaoh brushed him off again. God said to Moses, "Go back and tell Pharaoh to let My people go!" The result? Plague two: frogs. Plagues three, four, five…nine—"Go back; tell Pharaoh, 'Let My people go!'" God kept saying to Moses, "You have to go back; have enough faith to try again. One more time, go back and tell Pharaoh 'Let My people go!'" The result? Plague ten: death.

I can hear Moses saying to himself, *"Really? Another plague? You want me to go back… again?"*

Note that it was not until after the tenth plague that Pharaoh decided to let the Israelites go—victory! Like Moses, we have embodied the vision that our churches must become houses of prayer. We've followed God's directions, and we've *prayerfully* forced out spiritual robbers, made the proclamation, and have developed and implemented fruitful ministries. Yet, we've been rejected (attacked and distracted). God is also telling us to go back—go back and make the proclamation, "My house shall be called a house of prayer."

b. Three months after leaving Egypt (Exodus chapters 19-40) and at the base of Mount Sinai, God called Moses up into the mountain to receive instructions for the people—namely, the Ten Commandments. Their leader had been gone for an extended period of time, and the people sought a new leader. While Moses was on the mountain receiving the instructions, under the leadership of Aaron, the people were down in the valley disobeying those very instructions. God told Moses to go see what was happening. When Moses got down and saw what the people were doing, in anger, he threw down and broke the stone tablets inscribed with the Ten Commandments.

God himself had written the commandments on the tablets of stone, and His instructions were to place the tablets in the ark of the covenant (Exodus 25:16). God's directives were clear, and Moses had to go back. In faith, Moses went back up the mountain. He did not know what to expect from God when he went up; neither did he know what he would encounter when he came back down. As a result of trying again, the tabernacle was erected to house the ark, the tablets were placed inside, and God dwelled among them—victory! Moses had enough faith to give it one more try, and he experienced a *next-try* victory.

c. Too many times, we become faint and lose faith when victory is just within reach. Victory is in the next try! Go back and try again. You don't know what is going to happen; similarly, you may not realize victory if you don't try again. Joshua and his experience at Jericho (Joshua 6) is another example of a *next-try* victory. Moses was dead, and Joshua was the new leader of the children of Israel. Joshua was very successful in battle, and the other nations feared the Israelites.

Joshua's sights were now set on conquering the city of Jericho, but it was well-protected. The Lord told Joshua not to worry; the city was already defeated. God instructed Joshua to "…have your army march around the city once a day for six days. On the seventh day, I want you to march around the city seven times. Then, have all the people shout and the walls of the city will fall down." Joshua told the people what the Lord had instructed him to do, and they began to march.

Day one, the nation completely circled the city and nothing happened. Well, the walls were supposed to come down on the seventh day, so they tried again. Day two, after a complete circle around the city, nothing happened. Day three, four, five, and six—not even a crack appeared in the walls. Joshua had enough faith to try again, as instructed, on day seven. But I can see him looking at the walls for some evidence that the plan was working. Once, twice…five, six times around on day seven and zilch. Still, Joshua had enough faith to try again, and the walls of the city fell—victory! The *next-try* victory came as promised on the seventh day and seventh time around the city.

d. When God forecasts rain, grab your umbrella, put on your raincoat, get out your rain boots, and brace yourself because it's going to rain. It had not rained for three years, but God promised that it would (1 Kings 18:1). Elijah's confidence in God is very fascinating and equally astonishing at the same time. It had not rained for three years, and he had not yet prayed, but he was convinced enough to say, "…there is a sound of abundance of rain" (1 Kings 18:41, KJV).

In faith he prayed, expecting the abundance of rain, but nothing happened (1 Kings 18:41-43). I'm so thankful that prayer and faith are not single-use, disposable products. Elijah prayed again—still no rain. He prayed three, four, five, six times—no rain. Elijah is spiritually drained as his faith is confronted. His servant is physically exhausted after running to check for rain six times. Even so, he had enough faith to try again, and the report comes: "A cloud as small as a man's hand is rising from the sea" (1 Kings 18:44)—victory! Elijah had enough faith to give it one more try, and he experienced a *next-try* victory.

PRAYER AND FAITH ARE NOT SINGLE-USE,

DISPOSABLE PRODUCTS.

---

e. Like Moses, Joshua, and Elijah, Naaman had a *next-try* victory experience that forever changed his life. Naaman (2 Kings 5:1-14) was the commander-in-chief of Syria's army. He was also a leper. One day his wife's maid told her that Naaman would be healed of his leprosy if he would go to see the prophet in Samaria. His wife told him, he told the king, and the king told him to go and visit the prophet. With a letter of introduction from the king requesting that Naaman be healed of his leprosy and gifts of silver, gold, and suits, Naaman left for Samaria.

When the king of Israel read the letter, he was surprised by the strange request and thought that the king of Syria was trying to provoke him to battle.

When Elisha the prophet heard about the request and the king's response, he told the king to send Naaman to him. When he arrived at Elisha's home, Elisha sent a messenger to tell him to go and wash in the Jordan River seven times, and he would be healed. Naaman was upset that Elisha did not personally come out to see him and was equally offended by his instructions to wash in the dirty Jordan River. Persuaded, however, by his servants to follow Elisha's directions, Naaman went and dipped in the Jordan.

Scripture is silent as to Naaman's disposition and about the healing transformation after each dip in the Jordan River. I can only assume that he went down once and came up with no change. He went down a second, third…sixth time—no change. Looking at the dirty river and at his arms still showing signs of leprosy, it must have taken a tremendous amount of faith to try once more. A *next-try* victory was in the making; Naaman dipped for the seventh time and he was healed—victory!

f. I'm happy to report that *next-try* victories did not end with the conclusion of the Old Testament. In the New Testament, the story of the woman with the issue of blood is recorded (Mark 5:25-34). She had been sick for twelve years and had tried many doctors over the years; however, her health did not improve. In fact, her health was worse, and she had become poor from paying the doctors. She heard about another physician—Jesus—and decided to try again. She had enough faith to give it one more try and experienced a *next-try* victory. She thought to herself, *If I can just touch His clothes, I'll be healed.* She pressed through the crowd, touched Him, and the bleeding stopped—victory!

g. The New Testament also contains the story of the persistent widow (Luke 18:1-8). In this narrative, a widow came frequently to seek justice against someone who had harmed her. The judge was very godless and unfeeling and ignored her many attempts. Still, she had enough faith to try again. The judge could take it no longer and granted her justice—victory! Like this widow, we don't know if the next try will bring victory. Therefore, we must have enough faith to try again. I could go on, but I hope I've given you enough proof that it's worth it to try again. Even today, know that God is still in the *next-try* victory business.

Ride or Die

As I have already noted, there's something to be said about going back to hostile territory, early in the day because you still have work to do. Remember the story of Lazarus? Remember his illness, death, and resurrection (John 11)? Jesus gets the message that Lazarus is sick, but He delayed for two days. He finally decided to return to Judea to see about Lazarus, but his disciples were very concerned. "Teacher," the disciples answered, "just a short time ago the people there wanted to stone you; and are you planning to go back?" (John 11:8, GNT). Jesus decided to go back, despite their concerns, because He had work to do.

Not only did He make a conscious decision to go back to hostile territory, He went early in the day. This is powerful! His reasoning? Jesus said, "A day has twelve hours, doesn't it? So those who walk in broad daylight do not stumble, for they see the light of this world. But if they walk during the night they stumble, because they have no light." (John 11:9, 10, GNT). In other words, go back, go early, and do what you have to do while there's still light to avoid stumbling. His chief motivation for going back and for going back early is found toward the end of this narrative. Remember, Jesus had work to do, and here is the outcome: "Many of the people who had come to visit Mary saw what Jesus did, and they believed in him." (John 11:45, GNT).

In much the same way, our impetus for going back is to help reach souls for Christ. You've been attacked and distracted, you've walked away, the territory is still hostile, but are you willing to try again? Are you willing and ready to go back and die, if necessary, to assist God in reaching souls? Verse 16 will reveal whether or not you're a ride-or-die Christian. Thomas (called the Twin) said to his fellow disciples, "Let us all go along with the Teacher, so that we may die with him" (John 11:16, GNT). You may die, but die trying again.

GOD WILL POSITION YOU WHERE HE WANTS YOU,

BUT HE WILL NOT DEPLOY YOU UNTIL HE IS READY.

What do you have to lose? Absolutely nothing! Conversely, you have everything to gain. The risk in *not* trying again is far greater than the risk in trying again and again. Accepting your next assignment to cast/recast the vision, *prayerfully* drive out spiritual robbers, proclaim God's house a house of prayer, and to develop and implement fruitful ministries, could result in a *next-try* victory. Remember, God will position you where He wants you, but He will not deploy you until He is ready. The risk you take in *not* trying again is that you're likely to hear and experience God's pronouncement.

Reflections

_____

_____

_____

_____

_____

_____

_____

_____

_____

_____

_____

_____

_____

Reflections

Notes

1   Cymbala, p. 33.

EIGHT

A Formative Summary

B efore I address the subject of the pronouncement, allow me to provide a formative summary. In this case, a formative summary is an in-progress synopsis that will further shape our understanding of the progression a church will undertake to become a house of prayer.

House of Prayer Process

The process of becoming a house of prayer is a linear process; linear, meaning that the church (with the individual as the driver) will move from the vision to the prayerful removal of spiritual robbers to the proclamation, etc. (see Figure 10). But this linear movement does not mean that you will never elect to revisit a phase. As such, the process is linear (sequential) as it is nonconsecutive. In other words, moving to the next phase in the process requires you to honestly answer the question posed at each phase (e.g., Have you embodied the vision?). Still, it does not mean that you cannot and will not elect to straddle phases.

House of Prayer Process
© 2015 Bridge Ministries Consulting, Inc.
bridgeministriesinc.com

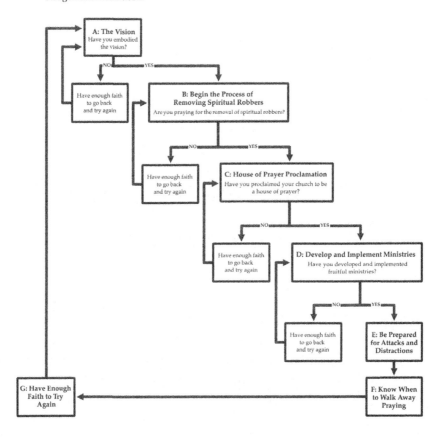

Figure 10. The House of Prayer Process[1]

In this linear process, it is also realistically feasible to be in two *appropriate* phases at the same time. God will guide you from phase to phase, but you must have the spiritual discernment to realize your need to revisit a phase, as necessary. For example, you may go back to fully embody the vision to help recast the vision, or you may go back to redouble your prayer efforts to remove spiritual robbers. Under such circumstances, revisiting a phase should not be seen as regression or as a failure. It does not imply that you did not honestly answer the questions posed (e.g., Are you praying for the removal of spiritual robbers?). Going back at this point is actually an indication of one's genuine desire to get it right.

While it is not encouraged and would not make sense to skip a phase (i.e., attempting to develop and implement fruitful ministries before God has given you a clear vision), there is no harm in regrouping and revisiting a phase. This subsequent reflection (phase straddling), however, is substantively different from when you initially transitioned through the process. As noted, if you did not get it right the first time, the process does call for you to have enough faith go back and try again.

REVISITING A PHASE SHOULD NOT BE SEEN
AS REGRESSION OR AS A FAILURE.

Because of the straddling that is likely to occur, I purposely used the word "phase" and not "step" to label each segment of the process. I am fully aware that a church (guided by an individual or group of individuals) could have moved to the next phase, but felt a spiritual need to revisit a former phase. Based on scripture and on my experience, you will move through the process in succession. Yet I can't say whether it will take six months for this church or 18 months for another since growth may demand phase straddling. Your experience will be different due to your own spiritual maturity and the spiritual maturity of your church. Again, it is a process based on spiritual discernment. As you pray, God will move you through the process.

House of Prayer Canvas

As Christians, we're often too passive when it comes to spiritual matters. Consequently, I believe that churches must be deliberate in implementing this process. You must be proactive in helping your congregation transition from simply being a church to become a house of prayer. The house of prayer canvas (see Figure 11) can be used to paint a picture of the strategy you'll use to help your church become a house of prayer. The seven phases of the process in transitioning from a church to a house of prayer can also be viewed as components that can either foster or impede a congregation's development in becoming a house of prayer. At the center of the canvas is the vision, which is where it all begins.

Requisites for Change (left side of the canvas) are components of the process that are necessary to occur before change can take place. These requisites include the prayerful removal of spiritual robbers, having enough faith to try again, and the proclamation. *Opportunities for Change* (bottom of the canvas) are components of the process that, when implemented properly, can afford your church a chance for success. These opportunities are proclaiming your church to be a house of prayer and developing and implementing fruitful ministries.

Threats to Progress (top of the canvas) are components of the process that can avert your congregation's movement toward becoming a house of prayer. These threats include spiritual robbers and the attacks and distractions you're likely to face. Finally, *Constraints to Progress* (right side of the canvas) are components of the process that have the potential to hold your church back. These constraints include attacks and distractions, having to walk away, and not taking the time to develop and implement fruitful ministries.

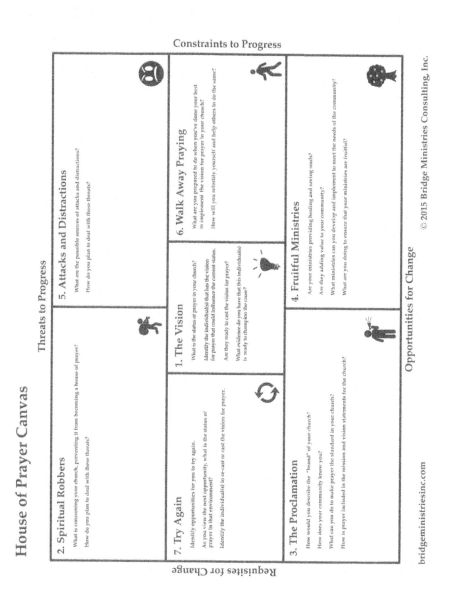

Figure 11. The House of Prayer Canvas[2]

Any attorney, police officer, or teacher will tell you that the right question is a powerful tool. Likewise, being able to provide a meaningful answer to the right question is an even more powerful tool. The right question can be effective, but a well-crafted response can be priceless. If you've ever watched congressional hearings, you know what I mean. The canvas used as a tool presents any church with questions that if answered meaningfully, within the context of your church, will yield invaluable responses to propel your church towards its goal of becoming a house of prayer.

The house of prayer canvas is a visual summary, and as noted, an influential tool. I encourage you to prayerfully consider the questions under each component of the process and use the canvas to challenge your church to become a house of prayer. These questions are not rhetorical and demand thoughtful responses if your church is going to become a house of prayer. Take the time and begin to paint the strategy, charting the course for profound spiritual growth in your church. Spiritual growth will always generate membership, physical, and financial growth. Eventually, it will yield kingdom growth.

THE HOUSE OF PRAYER CANVAS IS A VISUAL
SUMMARY AS WELL AS A TOOL.

---

1. The Vision
   - What is the status of prayer in your church?
   - Identify the individual(s) who has the vision for prayer that could influence the current status.
   - Is he/she ready to cast the vision for prayer?
   - What evidence do you have that this individual(s) is ready to champion the cause?

2. Spiritual Robbers
   - What is consuming your church, preventing it from becoming a house of prayer?

- How do you plan to deal with these threats?

3. The Proclamation
   - How would you describe the "brand" of your church?
   - How does your community know you?
   - What can you do to make prayer the standard in your church?
   - How is prayer included in the mission and vision statements for the church?

4. Fruitful Ministries
   - Are your ministries providing healing and saving souls? Are they adding value to your community?
   - What ministries can you develop and implement to meet the needs of the community?
   - What are you doing to ensure that your ministries are fruitful?

5. Attacks and Distractions
   - What are the possible sources of attacks and distractions?
   - How do you plan to deal with these threats?

6. Walk Away Praying
   - What are you prepared to do when you've done your best to implement the vision for prayer in your church?
   - How will you refortify yourself and help others to do the same?

7. Try Again
   - Identify opportunities for you to try again.
   - As you view the next opportunity, what is the status of prayer in that environment?
   - Identify the individual(s) to recast or cast the vision for prayer.

Spiritual Leadership and Implementation

The House of Prayer Process is biblical and the House of Prayer Canvas is structural, but at the end of the day, these concepts must be valued and prayerfully implemented to bring about the fundamental and predicted change. Let me be absolutely clear in what I'm expressing: your church will likely *not* become a house of prayer unless this process is esteemed by and executed under the headship of the spiritual leader. God can and will make it happen. Remember, it's inevitable and imminent, but we're not there yet. God is still expecting us to use our gifts, talents, and skills to assist Him in finishing His work. Accordingly, the spiritual growth we're seeking in our churches and the process I've outlined for us to get there cannot be accomplished without our spiritual leaders taking the initiative and purposefully leading their congregations through this process.

Like many of you, I've been blessed to have been associated with some great and some *not*-so-great organizations. The blessing in my association with the *not*-so-great organizations is that I was able to learn what *not* to do. I value those experiences because I can now identify effective leadership (or the lack thereof) that will engender positive organizational change. A specific type and level of intentional leadership is necessary in any organization to undertake any number of tasks that will guarantee success. Guess what? It's no different when we consider the type and level of leadership that is necessary to transition a church from simply being a church to a house of prayer.

TRUE SPIRITUAL LEADERS ARE RESPECTED
AND FOLLOWED BECAUSE OF
THEIR SPIRITUAL LEADERSHIP.

Spiritual leadership is one of the greatest wants of the current (modern-day) Christian church. It's not homiletical, theological, or administrative leadership that is most lacking. Unfortunately, for the membership and leaders alike, authentic spiritual leadership cannot be taught; it can only be developed prayerfully. I've discovered that individuals don't follow spiritual leaders because of their administrative or preaching skills. While administrative and preaching talent can help, true spiritual leaders are respected and followed because of their *spiritual* leadership.

As such, I'm challenging our spiritual leaders to take the lead in first valuing this house of prayer process and canvas and then championing the implementation of both to assist churches in transitioning from simply being a church to becoming a house of prayer. While implementation will consist of planning, meetings, and all the activities and tasks associated with organizational development, this is, first and foremost, a spiritual matter. Consequently, at the end of the day, you'll be judged by your ability to have moved the people spiritually, not by how well the church functioned organizationally or how well you preached.

Reflections

Notes

1   A poster size copy of *The House of Prayer Process* can be obtained at *www.BridgeMinistriesInc.com*

2   A poster size copy of *The House of Prayer Canvas* can be obtained at *www.BridgeMinistriesInc.com*

NINE

The Pronouncement

Seeing a fig tree by the road, He went up to it but found nothing on it except leaves. Then He said to it, "May you never bear fruit again!" Immediately the tree withered.

—MATTHEW 21:19 (NIV)

I've been privileged to sit at the feet of a few great preachers. One of the things I've observed and that I've been taught about preaching is that you always make an appeal. You're not finished until you've given someone the opportunity to accept Christ or to reconnect with Him. Why would you spend weeks preparing a sermon, take 40-plus minutes to deliver it, and not offer the listeners Christ? Why? Because too many of us only know *of* Christ, and we get caught-up and pre-occupied with activities to help others know *of* Him. Sadly, most of us don't *know* Christ; we only know *of* Him. Thus, the fundamental question is: who and what are we really offering to others?

Moreover, the appeal is not something you adlib at the end of a sermon. It is part of the sermon. It must be prayerfully considered and structured as you prepare. We need to remember that it is not about us—hearing "Amens" and ourselves preach—but about God using us to reach others. Since developing that understanding, I've never ended a sermon without an appeal.

When I preached what turned out to be my farewell sermon on January 28, 2006, I struggled as to how I was going to end the sermon; I did not have an appeal. I prayed and prayed, but God never revealed an appeal, or so I thought. That Sabbath, I requested that Matthew 21:12-18 be read for the scripture reading. The elder assigned to read the scripture did an excellent job. As requested, he read verses 12 through 18 and then, to my surprise, he continued reading and read verse 19.

As he began to read verse 19, I turned to the elder seated next to me and asked: "Why is he reading verse 19? I requested only verses 12 through 18."

I did not realize it because I was too busy playing pulpit police, but God had answered my prayer for an appeal. I preached the entire sermon, got to the end, and transitioned to the appeal as if it were in my notes. I remember sharing with the congregation my struggles over how to end the sermon, how the elder had added a verse, and how that additional verse was the foundation for the appeal. What an awesome revelation of God and His confirmation of this volume! That afternoon I reread Matthew 21:19, and the Holy Spirit took over.

I WAS TOO BUSY PLAYING PULPIT POLICE.

Trees, Leaves, and Fruit

As I stood before the congregation, the Holy Spirit revealed to me that the fig tree is a symbol of the church. The leaves on the fig tree represent the membership of the church, and the absent figs symbolize the lack of fruitful ministries. After the pronouncement, the withered state of the fig tree represents the current state of some of our churches—non-fruit bearing and dead (see Figure 12). Remember that Christ was hungry for He had work to do. He was trying to reach sinners, and He was looking to the church for assistance.

With that thought in mind, this is how Matthew 21:19 reads: *Seeing a church by the road, He went up to it but found nothing in it except church members. Then He said to it, "May you never bear fruitful ministries again!" Immediately the church died.* Unfortunately, Christ was unable to find fruitful ministries in the church to help in the end-time work of reaching sinners.

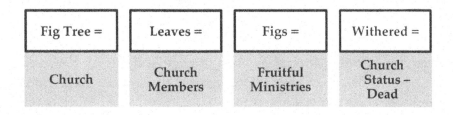

Figure 12. Pronouncement Elements

A *pronouncement* can be described as "a declaration, a verdict, a decree, or a judgment." In Matthew 21:19 (NIV) the pronouncement reads: "May you never bear fruit again! My prayer is that we (personally or our church) never hear that verdict or, if we happen to hear it, that the pronouncement is not directed at us. Similarly, I pray that we never experience that declaration. I pray that we will never have to worship in an environment where they are living out this pronouncement; that is, a non-fruit bearing and withered (dead) church.

When Jesus came to the fig tree (the church), He found it full of leaves (members), but no figs (fruitful ministries). The leaves were an indication of what should have been found on the fig tree. Well-flourishing fig trees are supposed to produce figs. "Fruit is a natural product. It grows without force; it is the free outcome of the plant."[1] In a similar way, a church with flourishing members should naturally produce fruit. Finding members in the church is an indication of what should be happening in the church. Through prayer, that church should have fruitful ministries in place to meet the spiritual, physical, emotional, and social needs of the church and community.

From a botanist's perspective, the flourishing green leaves were the result of roots that ran deep—the deeper the roots, the greener the leaves. In other words, in some churches there are long-time members who are planted deep into the soil of the church and community. Some of these members, however, are merely drawing nutrients and are not producing anything. I'm always amazed when I hear church members and leaders talk about how they've given their lives to the church. Yet from all that we observe, they've not given their hearts to Christ. These members, like the leaves on the fig tree, are green and attractive—an indicator of fruitfulness. However, these members are taking up space in the pews, using up precious resources, and not yielding fruit.

Instead of finding figs (fruitful ministries), all Jesus found were leaves (members). As it is natural to find a tree full of green leaves, there is absolutely nothing paradoxical about finding a church full of members. The larger questions include the following:

- What are the members doing?
- What is their focus?
- Have they developed and implemented fruitful ministries?

When Jesus gets to some of our churches, He'll find church members who are well-dressed, religious, self-focused, program-driven, and prayerless. In these churches, there is a form of godliness, but there is no spiritual substance, no spiritual intelligence, no spiritual enthusiasm, and no spiritual acumen.

Judgment and Spiritual Discernment

In making this observation about the state of some churches, one might be accused of passing judgment on the members and congregation. Nonetheless, I want you to take a look at Figure 13 and tell me which of the two trees is likely to produce fruit—better fruit. If I'm judging (my response is based purely on outward appearance), I would be more likely to say that Tree B would produce more fruit. When we judge, we place ourselves outside of and above the law. But James 4:12 (MSG) cautions us not to judge by asking the question: "Who do you think you are to meddle in the destiny of others?"

The only way anyone would really be able to tell which tree is likely to produce fruit is to wait for fruit to be produced. It will happen; we just have to be long-suffering and wait. When we wait, we're engaging in spiritual discernment. At this point we can become fruit inspectors. There are specific laws of nature that will determine if, when, and how much fruit a tree produces. When we *pre*determine that Tree A will not produce fruit or better fruit because of how it looks, we're placing ourselves outside of and above the laws of nature. We're judging; we're meddling in the destiny of others.

Tree A

Tree B

Figure 13. Fruit Inspection

While we're not to judge under the covering of spiritual discernment, we are called to be fruit inspectors. We may not like it, and at times, we actually shy away from doing it, but it is biblical. "You can identify them by their fruit, that is, by the way they act. Can you pick grapes from thornbushes, or figs from thistles? A good tree produces good fruit, and a bad tree produces bad fruit" (Matthew 7:16, 17, NLT). Our observations and conclusions about the fruitfulness or fruitlessness of Tree A or B should not be based on personal opinion of outward manifestations (judgment), but on the Word of God. Relax; I'm not judging you or your church. I'm humbly looking at your fruit juxtaposed to God's Word.

Oswald Chambers makes this powerful statement about the Christian's (our) response when engaged in fruit inspecting. He says the following:

> "When we discern that other people are not growing
> spiritually and allow that discernment to turn to criticism,
> we block our fellowship with God. God never gives us
> discernment so that we may criticize, but that we may
> intercede. The discernment God gives us is a prayer alert."[2]

Spiritual discernment calls for Christians to behave differently. That is, we must pray and wait until fruit is produced to reach conclusions and then continue in prayer. Sometimes a tree is not in its season; if we make judgments during the off-season, we could be wrong. This fig tree (church) in Matthew 21:19, however, was in its season, yet it still had no figs (fruitful ministries). The tree was inspected for fruit in its season and was found to be fruitless. That conclusion was not judgment, but fact. Again, under the covering of spiritual discernment and based on what is produced, our churches will be evaluated and characterized as being fruitful or fruitless—no spiritual substance, no spiritual intelligence, no spiritual enthusiasm, and no spiritual acumen.

SPIRITUAL DISCERNMENT CALLS FOR CHRISTIANS
TO BEHAVE DIFFERENTLY.

Withered Away

The church is at capacity and overflowing, but it does not produce much spiritual value. Unfortunately, when we're caught up in everything else but becoming a house of prayer, it does not allow us time to produce fruitful ministries. Consequently, we will hear Jesus' pronouncement: "May you never bear fruit again!" Matthew Henry notes, "Nothing is impossible with God, and therefore that what He has promised shall certainly be performed."[3] Many of our churches are already non-fruit bearing and withered (dead). We may not want to consider or acknowledge it, but many of them are living-out the judgment—"May you never bear fruit again!"

If God does not turn up the heat on the modern church, we will succumb to apathy, greed, lukewarmness, materialism, and the self-indulgence of the entertainment industry.[4] We will not be in any position to produce fruit. Accordingly, Jesus was direct, transparent, and resolute in His pronouncement. He said to the fig tree (church), you will never again produce any fruit; nothing will ever come out of you. Look around and you'll notice that some of our churches are withering away. Most of them are non-fruit producing and dead. We're withering away, and we don't even know it.

Brooklyn, New York, has a plethora of churches. No, really, the borough has an abundance of churches. On most blocks, you'll find several churches. Some, three or four in a row, others, right across the street from each other. On August 6, 2006, the Holy Spirit posed this question to me: how can a community have so many churches and still continue to have such a high level of violence, decadence, and crime? With that many churches, the spiritual saturation of Brooklyn should be at an all-time high. If McDonald's had that many restaurants clustered in any region, no other fast-food chain would stand a chance.

Accordingly, those churches should have such a spiritual monopoly on Brooklyn that the Devil would not stand a chance, right?

What I love about my Lord, first, is that He never asks rhetorical questions. His questions always demand an answer. Second, He also provides the answers to His questions. To answer this question, He took me to 2 Chronicles 7:14 (KJV): "If my people, which are called by my name, shall humble themselves, and pray, and seek my face, and turn from their wicked ways; then will I hear from heaven, and will forgive their sin, and will heal their land." In other words, the members in all of those churches are not praying. And those who are praying are not praying at a spiritually acceptable level. "Nothing but intense, believing prayer can meet the intense spirit of worldliness, which is complained of everywhere."[5]

Cyclic Praying

We often set aside 40 days, 2 weeks, 7 days, a special day, or specific hours for prayer. In too many of our churches prayer is an initiative (a cyclic program) when it should be a constant—a perpetual church pursuit. I don't have a problem with setting aside time for prayer; I'm more concerned with the unintended consequences. When we exclusively approach prayer (our approach to the throne of God) in this manner, we send the wrong message to our congregations. While it is not our intent, we send the message that now is the time you should *really* be praying and for how long. These prayer initiatives set unintentional limits on how long we pray and the intensity of our prayers and create a bipolar spiritual experience in our churches.

PRAYER INITIATIVES CAN CREATE A BIPOLAR

SPIRITUAL EXPERIENCE IN OUR CHURCHES.

I've witnessed the bipolar spiritual experience over and over again in many churches. Individuals and the collective church are on fire—a spiritual high—for 40 days or 2 weeks, and then they return to business as usual. We get to the end of the allotted time for prayer, and we stop praying. If it does not halt immediately, within a few weeks the amount and intensity of prayer wanes and stops. Over time we become conditioned to praying, stopping, and starting again. Now we're praying; now we're not. Accordingly, there is limited-to-no sustainability or continuity in such cycles of prayer for a church to develop and grow spiritually.

Furthermore, in our haste to organize these prayer initiatives, I've seen churches become distracted from the very act of praying. Instead of praying, we spend valuable time and energy trying to organize prayer. Too often the goal of praying becomes displaced with organizing prayer. This is called goal displacement. Do we really need to know who is praying, at what time, for how long, and about what? If we finally begin to pray, we become conditioned to praying passionately in cycles and quickly squander our spiritual high until the next time.

In defense of prayer initiatives, I've heard the argument that we set aside this time because of a special need in the church. Moreover, some members often direct my attention to the many miracles realized during the period of prayer: individuals got jobs, new converts, former members return, healings, etc. My retort has always been in the form of questions. "So absent the 40 days, we have no other special needs?" Any church can find a special need for the other 325 days of the year and as such, should be praying at a high level year-round. Second question: "If God can perform such miracles in 40 days, are we not limiting His blessings when we stop praying?"

That being said, I'm not opposed to a church's (or an individual) making a decision to pray for a specific number of days to launch their focus on prayer—becoming a house of prayer. It's for a specific purpose—not simply done to start the year, quarterly, or to end the year. You can decide to pray and fast for 7, 10, 21, or even 40 days to help focus the church on this most important initiative. All of these numbers have biblical significance. If you had to select a number of days to pray and fast, go with 40. Why? We have Jesus as our example.

To launch His ministry, Jesus spent 40 days and nights in prayer. What I find interesting is that after He started, scripture is silent as to His spending another specific large number of days in prayer again. Additionally, what we know from His example is that after the initial 40 days, He was consistently in prayer; He prayed always. Once you've gained the attention of the membership as it relates to prayer during the 40 days, avoid the highs and the lows, the bipolar spiritual experiences, and be persistent in prayer. You have to maintain the momentum.

> WE ALLOW THE DEVIL TO CALL A TIMEOUT;
> WE ALLOW HIM TO BREAK OUR FOCUS,
> STEALING OUR MOMENTUM.

I enjoy participating in and watching team sports—basketball, football, baseball. One of the things I've experienced and observed over the years is that when a team gains the momentum, they'll do all within their power to maintain that advantage. On the other hand, the opposing team usually calls a timeout, which is their attempt to disrupt the momentum. When we engage in a season of prayer and then stop praying, we relinquish the momentum gained during the season of prayer to the Devil. In some cases, we allow the Devil to call a timeout; we allow him to break our focus, stealing our momentum. Yet we expect God to do great things in our lives and in our church.

It's the same with anything in life, not just sports. If you gain something that's good for you, you do whatever is necessary to retain and maintain it. It's the same with prayer. What modern-day Christians fail to realize is that we've always held the advantage—the momentum. Our job, through incessant prayer, is to maintain that momentum. Prayer champions are fully aware that they have the advantage, and they do everything within their power to maintain it. They do whatever is necessary to keep the momentum.

What a radical change and spiritual benefit to our individual members and to the collective church and community if we were able to engender the same level of faithful prayer and expectancy of answers throughout the year, every year! Would it not be wiser to encourage our churches to develop a habit of prayer every day of the year? Churches cannot afford to focus on prayer for 40 days, 2 weeks, 7 days, special days, or specific hours exclusively. Prayer should be a daily experience that is accentuated when the collective church gathers throughout the week for worship. Daily intense prayer (absent the temporary highs and lows—the bipolar spiritual experience) must be a constant in the life of a church and the individual Christian.

Cut It Down

While your church may not be living out the pronouncement as yet, know that it's only because of God's unlimited grace and His abundant mercy. Many of our churches are living on borrowed time. What do I mean? Well, the narrative found in Matthew 21:19 was not the only time Jesus came to a fig tree (a church) and found no figs (fruitful ministries) on the tree (in the church). In Luke 13:6-9 (GNT) a man is conversing with his gardener about a fig tree.

> *"There was once a man who had a fig tree growing in his vineyard. He went looking for figs on it but found none. So, he said to his gardener, 'Look, for three years I have been coming here looking for figs on this fig tree, and I haven't found any. Cut it down! Why should it go on using up the soil?' But the gardener answered, 'Leave it alone, sir, just one more year; I will dig around it and put in some fertilizer. Then if the tree bears figs next year, so much the better; if not, then you can have it cut down."*

Now, I want you to read this parable again in the context of this chapter and the pronouncement elements (see Figure 12) ...

"There was once a man who had a church growing in his region. He went looking for fruitful ministries in it, but found none. So, he said to his gardener, 'Look, for three years I have been coming here looking for fruitful ministries in this church, and I haven't found any. Close it! Why should it go on using up the financial and human resources?' But the gardener answered, 'Leave it alone, sir, just one more year; I will focus the church by re-emphasizing the importance of prayer. Then if the church bears fruitful ministries next year, so much the better; if not, then you can have it closed."

Year after year, God has been coming to our churches looking for fruitful ministries, and unfortunately, He has found none. His command is swift and pointed: "Close it!" (cut it down!) After years of unfruitfulness, some of our churches are slated to be closed (cut down). These churches are continuing to consume resources that should be used otherwise to reach souls. Some of our churches are wasting God's financial and human resources. As such, God says, "Close it!" (cut it down!) Nevertheless, Jesus, in His mercy, has granted many of our churches a reprieve—one more year to get our act together. Accordingly, now is the time to move with spiritual urgency to begin the process of fruit bearing; don't squander this opportunity.

No Longer Needed

Back to Brooklyn, New York. Unfortunately, it is not Brooklyn alone. It is also happening in your community. Many churches throughout this country and others gather for worship on Sabbath mornings. We sing, we preach, and we pray, but not much is changing. We meet during the week for our assorted and numerous programs and activities, but much does not change. Next week we do it again. This pattern continues, week after week, month after month, year after year, and our "land" remains unhealed. "The single most important action contributing to whatever health and strength there is in our land is prayer."[6] The fig tree (church) is bursting with leaves (members), but there are no figs (fruitful ministries). Why? Well, many of these churches are living out the pronouncement. Hence, they are non-fruit bearing and withered—dead. Dead trees will eventually be cut down.

WE SING, WE PREACH, AND WE PRAY,

BUT NOT MUCH IS CHANGING.

Again, a fruit-bearing tree is supposed to bear fruit. But when it does not, the pronouncement is made: "Let no fruit grow on thee henceforward for ever" (Matthew 21:19, KJV). "Cut it down!" (Luke 13:6-9, GNT). The message is obvious, but we miss it. Christ is saying to us, "I no longer need you. You were planted in this region to bear fruit in this community, and you're not achieving that purpose. I don't need you anymore." There is a level of spiritual expectancy from those of us who gather regularly as a church that we produce fruitful ministries—not just ministries to placate the membership or to satisfy the ego of the spiritual leaders—but ministries that will allow us to meet the needs of God's people in these end-times and to finish this work.

Reflections

Reflections

Notes

1   Spurgeon, *Spurgeon on Prayer and Spiritual Warfare*, p. 482.

2   Jon Walker, *Growing with Purpose: Connecting with God Every Day* (Grand Rapids: Zondervan, 2009), p. 42.

3   Matthew Henry, *Matthew Henry's Commentary on the Whole Bible* (Peabody, Massachusetts: Hendrickson Publishers, 1991), p. 1722.

4   Sorge, p. 21.

5   Murray, p. 473.

6   Eugene H. Paterson, "Prayer As Public Good," *The Contemporaries Meet the Classics on Prayer*, ed. Leonard Allen (West Monroe, La.: Howard Publishing Company, 2003), p. 270.

Conclusion

You're likely saying to yourself: what now, and so what? Simply stated, *you* have to do it. *We* have to do it. We have to develop our churches into houses of prayer. The unintended consequences of the pronouncement are that another church is now *non*-fruit bearing and is not engaged in helping to finish the work. Here is the good news: a remnant number of churches remain that still have time to heed God's command to become a house of prayer. There is always good news in matters of spirituality. "Whenever people are willing to be led, the Lord is faithful to reveal what they should do at any particular moment."[1] If these remnant churches become houses of prayer, they will cause God to move in such a marvelous way that He'll be able to complete His work here on earth.

Accordingly, here is the summary of the process for becoming a house of prayer. You have to embody and cast the vision. After you've cast the vision that God's house must become a house of prayer, you have to begin the process of *prayerfully* removing spiritual robbers from His house. Next, you must proclaim your church to be a house of prayer. With this declaration, you'll immediately embark on the task of developing and implementing fruitful ministries. Know, however, that you're going to face attacks and distractions along the way. Consequently, you may have to walk away. Even so, walk away praying, knowing that you ought to have enough faith to try again.

Latter-Rain Praying

A weak spiritual life leads to a weak prayer life, and a weak prayer life leads to a weak spiritual life, and a weak spiritual life... I'm not trying to confuse you by taking you around and around, but this is the vicious cyclical experience for many individuals and of our churches. As we move through this cycle over and over like a hamster on a wheel, the Devil stands back and watches as we make no spiritual progress. Many of our churches are unequipped and unwilling to address this cycle.

In this state of spiritual blindness, we're unable to see the supernatural hand of God and so we're often too quick to take credit or to give credit for the things that God has done. Thus, we don't see the need for prayer, and we squander our prayer lives. Alas, we end up living in a perpetual state of prayerlessness. Prayerless Christians in the church of God are like paralyzed organs in the human body. Prayerless Christians handicap the vigor and life of the whole system.[2] In other words, prayerless Christians impede the proper functioning of the church. The two words "prayerless" and "Christian" should not be used to complement one another. The church is in danger when you or I don't pray, and that danger is exponentially multiplied as we approach the last days.

PRAYERLESS CHRISTIANS IMPEDE THE PROPER
FUNCTIONING OF THE CHURCH.

If the church had an occupation, it would be prayer. Similarly, if we would consider our vocation, we would see prayer prominently noted in the job title and used brazenly throughout the job description. One of the greatest challenges for spiritual leaders is to help their members understand the importance of prayer. If they were able to do this, they would have a successful church. God has shown me that prayer is the means to the end. As it was in the beginning, so shall it be in the end.

In other words, at the dawn of the church, the magnification of the Holy Spirit came as a result of prayer. Similarly, as we end the work, the intensification of the Holy Spirit will only come as a result of prayer. God began His great work of salvation through the apostles because they were willing to spend serious time with Him in prayer, and He will end that work through us—but only if we pray.

God does not need us, for His word is clear: "…if these should hold their peace, the stones would immediately cry out" (Luke 19:40, KJV). While He does not need us, He wants to include us in this end-time work. Many times, we fail to realize the opportunities we miss to contribute spiritually when we don't pray. "Who can say what power a church could develop and exercise if it would assume the work of praying day and night for the coming of the kingdom, for God's power, or for the salvation of souls."[3] As such, we must take our cue from the apostles. As they prayed for the "former" rain, we must pray for the "latter" rain. We must "… pray the Lord of the harvest to send out laborers into His harvest" (Matthew 9:38, NKJV).

Finishing the Work

Becoming a house of prayer is a means to the end, but it is not the end. E. M. Bounds puts it this way:

> *"Prayer is not an end in itself. It is not something done to be rested in, not something we have done, about which we are to congratulate ourselves. It is a means to an end. It is something we do that brings us something in return, without which the praying is valueless."*[4]

Consequently, becoming a house of prayer is not the end. We surrender all; we deny all to achieve the objective of becoming a house of prayer because it allows us to be co-laborers with Christ in finishing the work.

A praying person or church is an indication of change. When the Lord sent Ananias to restore Paul's sight after his Damascus-road experience (Acts 9:11-15), Ananias was extremely apprehensive about going because of Paul's history. God never addressed Ananias' concerns about being arrested, He simply said to him: "Go and do what I say" (Acts 9:15, TLB). Ananias had no cause for trepidation for God had already said, "He is praying to me right now…" (Acts 9:11).

Individuals who can be found praying are changed people. As such, others will be drawn to us. When we become houses of prayer and members of the community find us praying, it is an indication to them that things have changed. The community now knows that this place, our church, is no longer a place of commerce—good preaching, music, and programs in exchange for their love offering—but is now a place of prayer. A place where they can get their needs met.

Your church's becoming a house of prayer has tremendous consequences for those in your community who need to know Christ. When our churches become houses of prayer, we cultivate people of prayer (prayer champions). These individuals are able to delightfully represent God to our communities. They will frequently take the lead in witnessing to others—offering them salvation through Jesus Christ (see Figure 14). There is a method to God's ways. He knew that prayer was necessary to finish the work, and He knew that our churches—people of prayer—would play an important role in offering a sinner Christ. Hence, He stated, "…my house shall be called a house of prayer."

Figure 14. End-Time Work

Success in the Great Commission, "Go ye therefore, and teach all nations, baptizing them in the name of the Father, and of the Son, and of the Holy Ghost" (Matthew 28:19, KJV), cannot be achieved without prayer. I hope by now you have a clear understanding of the centrality of prayer in our work. When we attempt to implement the Commission before prayer, we engage in putting the cart before the horse. While in a practical sense, the horse can be persuaded to push the cart, it is not the most effective and efficient use of the horse's power!

It is the same with prayer and the Commission. Without prayer, the command to preach the Gospel to every creature can never be carried out.[5] We lose the power for optimal ministry when we launch the Commission before or without prayer. Where are we going? Who are we teaching and baptizing and in whose name? Notice that it says "…in the name of the Father, and of the Son, and of the Holy Ghost." How can we have the power of the Father, Son, and Holy Ghost without prayer? It will never happen.

There is work to be done. Prayer, becoming a house of prayer, is the primer, the prerequisite, and the precursor that is necessary to finish the work. As a carpenter cannot successfully complete his/her work without a hammer, likewise, God cannot successfully wrap up His work without a praying church. Moreover, you would not hire the carpenter if he/she did not have the requisite skills to complete the task. Why then would you expect God to employ you to complete His work if you're not praying?

GOD CANNOT SUCCESSFULLY WRAP UP HIS WORK
WITHOUT A PRAYING CHURCH.

Several years ago, I did the math and determined that most churches that I've attended or visited as an adult only engaged in corporate prayer for approximately 22 minutes each week. I was surprised by the number of minutes, as were others when I shared this fact publicly. Take a look at the week: Sunday through Saturday, and the opportunities and time made available for members to pray. The number of minutes at your church may be somewhat higher or lower, but do the math. Whatever the number, it is an indication of the worth we place on prayer. Knowing the important role of prayer, why would we expect

God to entrust His work to a church that only spends roughly 22 minutes per week in corporate prayer?

Let me be clear. I am not advocating for any specific quantity, for the process I've outlined is equally about the quality of our praying. Still the question must be asked: how much quality will we actually find in those 22 minutes? From both a quantity and a quality perspective, 22 minutes is all-together an inadequate amount of time for an *entire* congregation to spend in weekly corporate prayer, when prayer is the means by which a church gets its power. Again, I'm not endorsing an explicit number of minutes; I'm simply reporting what I've observed. There is a direct correlation between our spiritual weakness and our lack of corporate prayer.

The Prayer Meeting

"Prayer is represented in scripture as an essential factor in progress in the Christian life."[6] In other words, if you're not praying, you're not progressing as a Christian. Consequently, all those who are really seeking for communion with God will be seen in the prayer meeting.[7] Watchman Nee points out that prayer is a kind of service, which ought to be placed in a preeminent position.[8] Accordingly, prayer meetings should be the most important meetings in the church. Every spiritual leader should know that if the prayer meetings are neglected, all of his/her labors are in vain.[9]

One of the reasons we're spending so little time in prayer is because most of our churches don't have prayer meetings and those that do don't pray. "The prayer meeting has long been the step-child of the church."[10] As such, "prayer meetings seem to have lost their fervor, and are almost dead."[11] While members are usually enthusiastic about attending meetings for Bible study and other like ministries—they will find time for such meetings—when it comes to prayer meetings, the attendance is surprisingly marginal.[12]

Most churches usually don't have the same attendance issues Sabbath mornings, as they do on prayer meeting nights. We have enough scripture (Hebrews 10:25) to keep us in line on the Sabbath. However, scripture is somewhat silent when it comes to attendance and prayer meetings—this prayer-focused worship experience in the middle of the week. As such, we often feel some obligation to be at church Sabbath mornings but feel no such obligation for prayer meetings.

ATTENDANCE AT PRAYER MEETING IS USUALLY FROM A POSITION OF SACRIFICE.

Why is it that we make the sacrifice to attend church on Sabbath, while the same level of commitment is lacking in the middle of the week for prayer meeting? When I attend a church on Sabbath (the weekend) for worship, the church is full—in some cases, standing room only. These congregations usually worship in what can be described as their "main" sanctuary. I'm amazed, however, that when I return to the same church for prayer meeting, the worship is held in a chapel.

What's my point? Here it is: attendance at church on Sabbath is mostly from a position of obligation. Conversely, one's presence at prayer meeting is usually from a position of sacrifice. As with most things in life, the things we sacrifice for are usually the things we most value. I encourage you to make the sacrifice to be at prayer meeting, and you'll begin to value prayer or value it even more.

Since individuals attending prayer meeting are few in number, the programming efforts are minimal when compared to Sabbath— no musicians, no praise team, no worship leader, no bulletin, no order of worship. In some cases, the worship is planned that same evening. When our prayer meeting worship experience is treated as a second-class citizen, we're certain to get the current results— an unorganized worship experience that is poorly planned and attended. Without saying a word, the church signals the importance of prayer meeting to its members, visitors, and community.

For the few churches that are engaging their membership in prayer meetings, it's like going to math class and studying history. Don't get me wrong; there is a historical component to math, but history is definitely not math. The prayer meeting session should be—must be—about prayer. We need to stop the madness. We need to arrest this irrational development where prayer meetings are about everything else but prayer. "When it comes to de-emphasizing prayer and the prayer meeting in churches across the land, where are the spiritual results that prove we have found a better way?"[13] This quote is not meant to be a rhetorical question. This question demands an answer from the Christian community. How can we call ourselves Christians and have never known Christ to answer our prayers? That is the state of Christianity without the prayer meeting.

Spiritual Moments

Teachable moments are instances where lessons are learned in the casual moments of real life. Dr. Steven Carr Reuben notes that, as a parent or teacher, one of the most important skills to nurture is the ability to recognize and capitalize on "teachable moments" in every-day life.[14] Like teachable moments, there are "spiritual moments" that must be recognized and capitalized on because of their value. For instance, spiritual moments are those moments during church worship experience when we get a chance to plant a seed of prayer in the church and to lay a foundation for the church to become a house of prayer.

In our church worship experiences, we frequently miss those opportunities. We're too busy sticking to and with the script (the order of worship) that we don't recognize and capitalize on the moment. There are prayer lessons to be learned in those real-life moments, and we fail to notice them. The Lord presents us with a spiritual moment—an opportunity for our spiritual leaders to take us a little higher—and we neglect to take advantage of it. As a result, we often end up with 22 minutes of corporate prayer.

"Oh, we're having church today." "This is a beautiful worship service." "Didn't our hearts burn?" It's amazing; while I've heard these affirmations repeated many times at church because of the choir or soloist's performance or because of a powerful sermon, I've never *really* heard similar claims regarding the spirit of prayer at church. Why? We're often too casual with these spiritual moments. In some of our churches, we do everything else on Sabbath and neglect to allocate ample focused and meaningful time for prayer. Then we turn around and launch a prayer line or website to take prayer requests.

Think about it; we don't do the children's story time online. We don't forgo collecting tithes and offering *in* church and do it solely online. Again, we don't sacrifice the choir or soloist selection and air it online. We have the technology, but we don't. Prayer, however, is one of the only activities that gets shortchanged at church and is then organized online (via phone or web).

These online activities should be a natural extension of what happened on Sabbath morning, afternoon, and/or at our prayer meetings. Too often, however, the prayer line, etc. becomes the nucleus of our corporate prayer activities. How foolish is it to have a captive audience at church, abandon doing your main thing, and then expend additional resources to build a captive audience online to do your main thing? This way of thinking and operating defies logic.

WE'RE BEING ROBBED SPIRITUALLY OF A BLESSING,

AND WE DON'T EVEN REALIZE IT.

Most individuals and churches are so accustomed to not praying that we don't know the difference. Prayerlessness is normal. We're being robbed spiritually of a blessing, and we don't even realize it. Unwittingly, we've allowed ourselves to be used by the Devil, and we've removed prayer from the center of our churches and have placed it on the periphery or semi-periphery. Prayer is more often than not a secondary thought. Prayer, instead of being our first option, is habitually the third or fourth alternative. When we engage in this type of prayer behavior, it becomes the norm.

Paradigm Shift

Regrettably, the prayerless church has become the model for us, and we're likely to bequeath the same for generations to come. What we're witnessing today in our churches and in society at large is that legacy of prayerlessness. Several years ago, some of our great-grandparents, grandparents, and parents marginalized prayer in their homes and churches. If you've come this far in reading this book and you've overlooked it or have forgotten, let me clear it up and/or remind you that this is exactly what the merchants and customers were doing when Jesus cleared the temple. Today, some of us are continuing the same practice of marginalizing prayer, and we're in danger of transferring that same legacy to our children unless something changes.

The consequences of this legacy of prayerlessness are non-fruit-bearing, withered, dead churches. Such churches are useless to God. As a result, a paradigm shift is needed if we're going to be of any value to God in helping Him to finish this work. A *paradigm* is "a framework containing the basic assumptions, ways of thinking, and methodology that are commonly accepted by members of a scientific community."[15] The related concept—a *paradigm shift*—is "a radical change in the basic assumptions, ways of thinking, and methodologies linked to that framework." As a spiritual community, a paradigm shift is needed in our assumptions, ways we think about, and in our approach to prayer.

As a start, the following are a few proposals your spiritual leader can implement to begin the shift in your church:

a. We need to come to the indisputable understanding that the church's primary function, first and foremost, is to be a house of prayer. If the church fails at that, it will eventually fail at everything else.

b. We need to cultivate and maintain an organizational culture and worship structure where consistent corporate and personal prayer is the norm.

c. We need to acknowledge that there is a process to becoming a house of prayer, but the process itself is meaningless if we're not praying the length of the way.

d. Any new pastor to a church should spend the first 52 weeks of his tenure preaching and teaching about prayer. Doing this will set the tone for the congregation and unleash a tremendous wave of power to move that church forward spiritually. They should also spend an hour or two each week "unpacking" each sermon with the members and visitors.

e. The weekly bulletin that outlines your Sabbath worship should also include the plans for prayer meeting and other prayer experiences (prayer line). Members and visitors should know what to expect each week for prayer meeting, etc.

f. Select a book on prayer and read it with your congregation each quarter. This will strengthen the prayer life of your members and visitors and build their library.

g. Implement the use of prayer request cards and a prayer box.

h. Every Sabbath, after worship, gather the congregation for prayer—spend 30 minutes in prayer after worship each week.

i. We use available communication technology to share almost everything—often too much. Use the available technology (print, website, social media, etc.) to share in a systematic and consistent way the prayer needs of your church and members.

j. We need to equip spiritual and departmental leaders with the necessary tools to systematically implement the process to become a house of prayer—tools that will assist their church in achieving God's goal for His last-day church, finishing the work.

k. Our spiritual leaders must appreciate the consequences of being spiritually prepared before they stand before God's people. They must develop a profound understanding of the connotation between their time spent in prayer, spiritual preparedness, and their success in the pulpit, etc.

l. Like President Bush's educational platform "No Child Left Behind" of several years ago, we need to ensure that every member in our church is engaged in intercessory prayer.

m. We should have a burden for prayer without making prayer a burden. Too many of our churches make prayer a burden for their membership. We're too busy trying to teach them *how* to pray instead of teaching them *to* pray. We need to start treating our members like adults instead of children when it comes to prayer. We need to stop planning for prayer and start praying.

n. Time must be made for a season of prayer at the beginning and end of every ministry. I'm not referring to the obligatory opening prayer and closing prayer. I'm talking about setting aside a considerable portion of time that will allow participants to realize the relationship between the success of the ministry and their praying. I recently came across this church sign (see Figure 15) and was very encouraged. Notice the statement at the bottom.

o. We need to reverse the legacy of prayerlessness by institutionalizing prayer among our children. We must lay the foundation and sow the seeds for prayer by helping our children learn how to pray with and for each other.

Figure 15. Church Sign

The Church's Primary Function

The list above is not exhaustive; neither do I have the space or time to elaborate on each suggestion. But the essential feature in achieving the paradigm shift in our assumptions, ways we think about, and in our approach to prayer, is grasping the role of the church. The church's primary function, first and foremost, is to be a house of prayer. If the church fails at that (being a house of prayer), it will eventually fail at everything else. Hold on, allow me to make my point.

There is another sociological theory called Structural Functionalism, which is also known simply as Functionalism. Functionalism is one of the three main sociological perspectives. The theory proposes that all aspects of a society serve a function and are necessary for the survival of that society. "According to functionalism, an institution only exists because it serves a vital role in the functioning of society. If it no longer serves a role, an institution will die away."[16] In other words, if churches are no longer serving their role in our society, they will die. If they serve no function, they will evolve out of existence.[17]

In our current sociopolitical and socioeconomic climate, individuals are looking to the Christian church to address the problems in our society. As such, the question Christians must ask is: what is the function of the church? While the Christian church has played many roles since its development, it's done a poor job of executing its primary function—being a house of prayer—at the expense of those other roles. The primary function of the church is to be a house of prayer. In that role, it is to provide a safe environment where individuals can develop a relationship with Christ through prayer. So the church is to provide every opportunity for us to develop that relationship with Christ, accept Him as Lord and Savior, and then to share that experience with others. All of this is made possible through prayer.

If, for example, while performing this primary function—being a house of prayer—injustice is encountered, the church has a responsibility to appoint individuals, provide resources as needed, provide a forum, etc. to address said concerns. However, its primary function cannot be to merely fight injustice. The church is not and was never intended to be a civic organization, a social club, a social service agency, etc. When the church becomes a civic organization, for example, it loses its power for effective ministry—the salvation of souls. Remember Acts 6:3 and 4, which says, "…appoint men over this business. But we will give ourselves continually to prayer, and to the ministry of the word." When the church is distracted from its primary function, we end up with amazing activists and average Christians.

Christ was an activist, but He was a Christian first. An amazing prayerless activist, who is not first a Christian, is no good to himself or to his community. We often reject Christ by the way we practice Christianity, and then we wonder—we're even surprised—when we don't get answers to our prayers. When we don't use things as designed, we often don't get the maximum benefit from them. Guess what? We're not getting the maximum benefit from Christianity—namely, our churches. Our communities are unchanged and will remain unchanged until we incorporate Christ. I'm not talking about including Christ how *we* decide to include Him, but about including Christ in such a way that churches are allowed to fulfill their primary function.

Most Christians have never connected the following two scripture passages. The first statement was made by God in the Old Testament: "Let them make me a sanctuary; that I may dwell among them" (Exodus 25:8). The second statement was made by Jesus in the New Testament: "And said unto them, It is written, My house shall be called the house of prayer" (Matthew 21:13). We're reminded in Matthew, by Jesus, that the sanctuary (My house), was commissioned by God in Exodus to be a house of prayer. Okay, what about the connection? Here it is: the "sanctuary" in Exodus, the "My house" in Matthew, and our modern-day church are all one and the same and designed to be a place of prayer.

Imagine that you have a home, and family members and/or friends came to visit with you. What is the *primary* means by which you'll engage those visitors? The answer? Conversation, of course. Through conversation, you'll show them the house, find out what they'd like for dinner, discover places they'd like to visit, etc. You'll communicate with your house guests by talking. Well it's no different when it comes to our churches. God said: "Let them make me a sanctuary that I may dwell among them." God wants to hang out with us at church. As with our family members and friends, when God shows up, what is the *primary* means by which we'll engage Him? The answer? Prayer. Through prayer, we'll share our joys and our concerns with God. We'll communicate with Him by praying.

THE PRIMARY FUNCTION OF THE CHURCH IS TO
ENGAGE A GOD WHO WANTS TO DWELL AMONG US.

In the context of functionalism and the two previous passages, the primary function of the church is to engage a God who wants to dwell among us. By becoming a house of prayer, we'll realize our primary function, which is the catalyst for the paradigm shift. Herein is the functionality of the Christian church and prayer. Now that I've presented my observations, let me say it again: the church's primary function, first and foremost, is to be a house of prayer. If the church fails at that function, it will eventually fail at everything else. Ultimately, that church will be told to bear no more fruit, be cut down, or it will evolve out of existence.

Promises, Promises

If you're not praying, you're limiting and delaying God. You're limiting God in blessing the church, you, and others. Similarly, you're delaying His work. If God said it and you sincerely pray for it, He will do it. Too many times, however, we limit God by constraints

148

we place on Him because of our unbelief and sins. Why would God give us anything we don't believe that we're going to get? Unbelief hinders prayer and blocks the fulfillment of promises made.

Similarly, God can't bless us when we're disobedient (Psalm 66:18).

> *"Jesus made some fantastic promises regarding prayer, but He was speaking to those whose hearts were beating in unison with His own. He never intended to make Himself subject to the whims of just anyone who might happen to read His words."*[18]

While we limit Him with unbelief and sin constraints, we also attempt to manipulate Him by forcing our way around His will for us and for His church.

God wants our churches to be houses of prayer. He is the primary stakeholder in the matter and has guaranteed it. He wants it and has assured it, and we need to ask for it. Holding God to His word means that if you pray, God will move. In other words, when you pray, He moves. He moves not because of your prayer, but because of His promise. Too many of our modern prayers are in vain because we approach God, imagining that we have some claim upon God whereby He is under obligation to answer our prayers.[19] We would do well to remember that we're owed nothing by Omnipotence and have no claim on anything except as Jesus offers it.[20] There is no power in your prayer beyond what He has promised to do. Your prayers will never cause Him to move outside of His will—He has never promised to move outside His will.

In Ezekiel 36:37 (TLB), the Lord God says:

> *"I am ready to hear Israel's prayers for these blessings and to grant them their requests. Let them but ask, and I will multiply them like..."*

In prayer, we can hold God to His word. If He said it and we pray it, He will do it. What other authority allows us such a guarantee? God is standing by to hear and respond to your prayers. He is willing to support us in doing the uncommon in common ways. He is ready to assist us in making the paradigm shift. He is ready to position us to assist Him in this end-time work. He is ready to help us in the transition from church to house of prayer. The ball is in our court, however, to ask for these blessings. So many promises in the Bible are related to praying and receiving, yet we refuse to pray.

The same promise Jesus made to the disciples at the Last Supper is available to us in these last days. He said:

> *"I tell you the truth, anyone who believes in me will do the same works I have done, and even greater works, because I am going to be with the Father. You can ask for anything in my name, and I will do it, so that the Son can bring glory to the Father. Yes, ask me for anything in my name, and I will do it"*

> —JOHN 14:12-14, NLT

Christ promised His disciples that they would be able to do even greater works than He did. Well, what works, exactly, did Jesus actually do while here on earth? He called and trained disciples, taught, fed thousands, calmed storms, walked on water, blessed others, healed, cast out demons, and He raised the dead to life. Wow! Now you're asking yourself, can we really do even greater works than Christ did? Is this really possible? The answer to both questions is yes.

The promise to do even greater works, however, was conditional. First, they had to believe. Second, He had to be present with His Father. Third, they had to ask. And fourth, the work had to bring God glory. All that?! At first glance, one might recoil in fear of failure because of all the conditions. Don't! One of the conditions has already been met; He is with His Father. Check.

As He sits at the right hand of the Father, He merely requests that we believe in Him and ask for anything that will bring glory to God. Is it really that straightforward? Can we really do even greater works than Christ? Yes! How is that possible? Well, we live in a greater world in greater need of greater works. Herein is the formula that will change this world: a group of believers become a house of prayer and cry out to their Father in heaven for power to do works that will bring Him glory. This is a miracle factory that knows no limits. Hold on to your seats; we have not witnessed anything yet! The promise is sure: "I will do it!" Yet the only way for even greater works to occur is for us to cultivate prayer.

Notice that the only required condition Jesus repeated twice is for us to ask—to pray. Why did Jesus repeat Himself? Because He knew that some of us would attempt to do even greater works without praying. It's as if He knew we would be somewhat weak when it came time to pray, so He repeated Himself—"Yes, ask…" God always has our best interest at heart. Consequently, we have no reason to doubt when praying; God has doubly promised to answer—"I will do it."

Deceptive Satisfaction

I've been a Christian all of my life, and if our current way of living and status is it, then I give up, and I encourage you to do the same. This can't be it. In fact, this is *not* it. An awesome amount of power that we know about and have yet to fully experience is available to us. In 2004, I stumbled upon that power, and I want to experience more of it. That is why I now live. Sadly, we're threatened by a dangerous wave of misleading satisfaction in our churches. Because of the prayers of a faithful few, the latter rain is being poured out. But it is being poured out in *measure,* and we're mistakenly satisfied.

WE'RE WICKEDLY SATISFIED WITH THE ORDINARY
WITHOUT CHALLENGING OURSELVES
FOR GREATER RESULTS.

How many times have you heard a statement that goes something like this? "If one soul comes to Christ as a result of this service, program, or activity, it would have been worth the effort expended." While this statement is completely true, it is also full of low expectations and mediocrity. It is an argument based on us being wickedly satisfied with the ordinary without challenging ourselves for greater results. We're satisfied with the one soul when God is ready, willing, and able to save one thousand per day.

The other argument I've heard over the years is the "You-don't-know" argument—you don't know who this ministry is reaching. I'm fully aware that we will be involved in ministries where we don't know how it's impacting spiritually on others. But I'm also fully convinced that, at some point, the God that I serve will provide me with some evidence (tangible fruit) of my co-laboring with Him. How terrible of God to make us labor week after week, month after month, year after year, without any encouragement through the evidence of changed lives to keep us excited about laboring.

Ministries are designed to bear fruit, and the evidence of fruit encourages us to till the soil and plant again. I reference, once again, the parable found in Luke 13:6-9. The owner of the vineyard came year after year looking for figs (fruit)—some return on his investment and labor. He came looking for a harvest, evidence that his labor was not worthless. The gardener (Jesus) was willing to put in the additional work for another year because He trusted that the tree would eventually bear fruit; it was expected. No farmer would continue to plant if he never got a yield.

Similarly, God has called us to be fishers of men (Luke 5:10). Think about it. What fisherman would continue to fish if he never caught anything? He would abandon that vocation in favor of one producing results—fruit. The formula is very straightforward: follow Christ's instruction to let down your net (Luke 5:4), catch fish, and be encouraged to fish again. Why would God call us to be fishers of men, ask us to prayerfully develop and implement fruitful ministries, and expect us to continue fishing week after week, month after month, year after year, without a catch? The catch is the evidence that He is blessing our efforts. That's not the kind of God that we serve. Why would you continue to fish if He were? We're not willing to spend the time in prayer to understand His will and plan for us and our churches. As a result, we forfeit the blessing of additional souls.

I'm challenging us to arise from this benumbing state of counterfeit satisfaction and pray. Without prayer, we will only have success in measure, but we will never experience success in abundance. "How difficult it seems to be for the church to understand that the whole scheme of redemption depends on people of prayer. How strange that instead of learning this simple and all-important lesson, the modern church has largely overlooked it.[21] The salvation of this earth hangs squarely on our praying; yet we're of limited use to God in finishing the work. We're not saved, and we're at peace. We're in no position to lead others to Christ, and we're unmoved. We're not praying, and we're content.

WE HAVE A FIXED QUANTITY OF TIME THAT'S ON THE VERGE OF RUNNING OUT.

Sometimes we are so busy doing all kinds of things for God that we forget to enjoy time with Him in prayer. When we are too busy to pray, we really are too busy to be Christians.[22] Who or what is it that has you so busy in life or at church that you can't pray? Who or what has you so preoccupied that you're willing to risk your own eternal safety? Ellen. G. White points out that no man or woman is safe for a day or even an hour without prayer.[23]

Avoid the pronouncement in your life and in the life of your church to never bear fruit again. When it comes to matters of prayer, we must stand up and cast-off this synthetic euphoria of satisfaction. If we're attending church week after week and we're going around calling ourselves Christian, it's time for us to get real and practical about prayer and finishing God's work. No more excuses. We have a fixed quantity of time that's on the verge of running out. I don't know when that time is, but I know it will run out soon.

Embody the vision and prayerfully challenge your church to become a house of prayer. As you embody the vision, you'll begin to see scripture and life through the lenses of prayer. It's an amazing process of spiritual revelation concerning God, things related to prayer, and the overall importance of prayer in the life of a Christian. "It is written, My house shall be called a house of prayer." It must happen, and it will happen very soon; *it's inevitable, and it's imminent.*

Reflections

Reflections

Notes

1   Jim Cymbala, *Breakthrough Prayer* (Grand Rapids: Zondervan, 2003), p. 207

2   Bounds, p. 553.

3   Murray, p. 382.

4   Bounds, p. 241.

5   Murray, p. 655.

6   J. Oswald Sanders, *"Praying in the Spirit,"* *The Contemporaries Meet the Classics on Prayer*, ed. Leonard Allen (West Monroe, La.: Howard Publishing Company, 2003), p. 196.

7   Ellen. G. White, *Steps to Christ* (Hagerstown, Md.: Review and Herald Publishing Association, 1977), p. 98.

8   Nee, p. 112.

9   Charles Finney, *"The Purpose of Public Prayer,"* *The Contemporaries Meet the Classics on Prayer*, ed. Leonard Allen (West Monroe, Louisiana: Howard Publishing Company, 2003), p. 207.

10 Sue Curran, *The Praying Church: Principles and Power of Corporate Praying* (Lake Mary, Florida: Creation House Press, 2001), p. xii.

11 Clifford O. Gyanifi, "Maintaining a Vibrant Prayer Meeting: Steps to help keep your members alive," *Adventist World* (April 2007), p. 22.

12 Nee, p. 112.

13 Cymbala, *Breakthrough Prayer*, p. 23.

14 Steven Carr Reuben, *Children of Character: Leading Your Children to Ethical Choices in Everyday Life* (Santa Monica: Canter & Associates, 1997), p. 123.

15 *http://dictionary.reference.com/browse/paradigm?s=t*

16 *https://www.thoughtco.com/functionalist-perspective-3026625*

17 William J. Chambliss and Daina S. Eglitis, *Discovery Sociology Second Edition* (Thousand Oaks, Calif.: Sage, 2016), p. 18.

18 George Vandeman, *Unlocking Heaven's Storehouse* (Thousand Oaks, Calif.: It Is Written, 1980), p. 25.

19 R. A. Torrey, *How to Pray* (Chicago: Moody Publishers, 2007), p. 47.

20 Bill Knott, "Realigned by Prayer," *Adventist World* (September 2014), p. 3.

21 Bounds, p. 566.

22 Frank Hasel, *The Holy Spirit and Spirituality: Adult Sabbath School Bible Study Guide* (Nampa, Ida.: Pacific Press Publishing Association, 2017), p. 51.

23 Ellen. G. White, *The Great Controversy* (Boise, Ida.: Pacific Press Publishing Association, 1950), p. 530.

My Prayer

To end my farewell sermon, I courageously told the congregation that I had to walk away. I told them that while I didn't know where God would take me, I knew that wherever He did lead me, I had to have enough faith to try one more time. I'm walking away, but I'm walking away *praying*. I closed with this prayer:

Father, into Your hands we commit our church. Your word is clear; Your house shall be called a house of prayer. You've shared with me that it is inevitable, and it is imminent. It will happen, and it will happen soon. But You've just revealed to me that there are some churches that are not bearing fruit. In Your wisdom, You will say to those churches, "Wither up and bear no fruit ever again." Lord, my sincere prayer, today, is that that will not be Your pronouncement on this church.

Lord, there is a work to be done on this corner. There is a work to be done in this vineyard. But You need a house of prayer in which to do it. Fruitless ministries, we know, Lord, will not do it. You need people who are committed to prayer. You need people who are sold out to prayer. You need people who will wear themselves out in prayer.

So my prayer, today, is that You will hold back the winds of strife from this church. Hold back the pronouncement of withering, dying, and bearing no fruit. Hold it back, Lord, please. You have to do it. We have to assist You prayerfully in finishing this work.

Father, I end this prayer by thanking You for the time we've spent together. Your house will be a house of prayer. It's inevitable and imminent. Our role is to allow You to use us. I pray that we will be able to do that. This is our prayer, in Jesus' precious name. Amen.

House of Prayer Indicator Assessment

Welcome to an assessment that has the potential to grow the spirituality of your church and change your life for the better.

Some church leaders and members have been duped into removing prayer from the center of their churches and have placed it on the periphery or semi-periphery. In these churches, prayer is not valued and prayerlessness is the norm. What about your church? Is prayer a priority in your church? Is your church a house of prayer?

This assessment is a tool you can use to help assess the status of prayer in your church. By completing the assessment you'll gain insight into whether your church is a house of prayer. Hold on to your seat; it'll confirm or challenge your beliefs about your church's prayer status.

The assessment is divided into two parts. **Part I** has four sections and **Part II** has four sections. The assessment will take approximately 20 minutes to complete. You'll be presented with statements. Indicate the extent to which you agree or disagree with each statement by using the following options: **Strongly Agree, Agree, Disagree,** or **Strongly Disagree.** You'll also be presented with questions. Answer **Yes** or **No** to each question.

It is important that you respond truthfully and from your perspective and not try to provide answers that you think others would like to hear. The objective is to get a true status of prayer in your church, from your point of view.

The journey to spiritual change begins now! Ready to get started?

PART I				
Section One	**Strongly Agree**	**Agree**	**Disagree**	**Strongly Disagree**
Prayer is the fundamental biblical principle that should guide a church's activities (its ministries and programs).				
The church's prayer life (its commitment to prayer) can positively impact the surrounding community.				
The level of spiritual growth in a church can be strengthened through corporate prayer.				
Prayerless Christians (church members) can impede the proper functioning of a church.				
A prayer strategy should lead the spiritual, membership, and financial growth strategy for a church.				

Section Two	**Yes**	**No**
Is there a spiritual environment in your church that supports prayer and prayer related activities?		
Does your church have a prayer champion(s), i.e., someone with a profound understanding of the importance of prayer in God's house (your church) and supports it?		
Does your church view individuals, practices, and/or things that are hindering its spiritual growth and development as a threat?		
Is your church recognized by the community as a place of prayer?		
Is the attendance at prayer meeting worship service significantly lower, when compared with other worship services?		

Section Three	Strongly Disagree	Disagree	Agree	Strongly Agree
Cultivating and maintaining an organizational culture and worship structure where consistent corporate and personal prayer is the norm, is practiced at my church.				
In my church, prayer plays a prominent role in the lives of members and chiefly in the lives of church leaders.				
My church is not simply going through the motions, and focuses on genuine prayer and worship, week after week.				
My church does not need to change its assumptions, ways of thinking about, and approach to prayer.				
My church's primary function, first and foremost, is to be a house of prayer.				

Section Four	Yes	No
Is prayer worship?		
If your church were to schedule a prayer meeting service and a game night, would the attendance at game night be better?		
Is prayer included in the mission and vision statements of your church?		
Are the church's ministries adding spiritual value to the community?		
Does your church spend quality time in prayer at committee and planning meetings?		

PART II				
Section Five	**Strongly Disagree**	**Disagree**	**Agree**	**Strongly Agree**
I think prayer, as a central worship practice, has been removed from the center of my church.				
The legacy of prayerlessness in my church is negatively impacting our surrounding community.				
I've witnessed that there is a correlation between my church's spiritual weakness and its lack of corporate prayer.				
Prayerless Christians (church members) are impeding the proper functioning of my church.				
A prayer strategy is not leading the spiritual, membership, and financial growth strategy for my church.				

Section Six	**Yes**	**No**
Is the level of unity (oneness, one accord) great among members at your church?		
In your church, is more time allocated for Bible study, singing and/or preaching, when compared to time spent praying?		
In your church, are the youth and children excited about prayer?		
Do all of the worship services in your church reflect prayer as a priority?		
Are there individuals, practices, and/or things in your church preventing it from moving forward spiritually?		

Section Seven	Strongly Agree	Agree	Disagree	Strongly Disagree
Churches should cultivate and maintain an organizational culture and worship structure where consistent corporate and personal prayer is the norm.				
Prayer must play a prominent role in the lives of church members and chiefly in the lives of church leaders.				
Churches should avoid the pitfall of simply going through the motions, week after week, when it comes to genuine prayer and worship.				
Churches that are serious about prayer, usually change their assumptions, ways of thinking about, and approach to prayer.				
The church's primary function, first and foremost, is to be a house of prayer.				

Section Eight	Yes	No
During the last 3 months, have you preached or heard your pastor preach a sermon on prayer?		
Does your church have a weekly prayer worship service where prayer, and only prayer, is the focus?		
Are your members and visitors excited about prayer?		
Does your church have and use prayer request cards and/or a prayer box?		
Does your church have a vision for prayer (i. e. a clear awareness of what can and will happen when you and other members pray)?		

You've completed our House of Prayer Indicator Assessment. Thank you for valuing your church and for investing your time in completing the assessment.

Please refer to the scoring grid (pages 168-171) to calculate your assessment summary score. For example, Part I, Section One, first statement: if you responded "Strongly Agree" give yourself 2.5 points, etc. Similarly, Part I, Section Two, first question: if you responded "Yes" give yourself 2.5 points, etc.

Total your score from each section and insert the value on each line below. Finally, add the totals from each section together for your assessment summary score. Summary scores for our House of Prayer Indicator Assessment can range between 20-100.

(1) ___ + (2) ___ + (3) ___ + (4) ___ + (5) ___

+ (6) ___ + (7) ___ + (8) ___ = ___

This score indicates that you believe your church is at:

- **Level Five (90-100):** *Steadfast and assertive*

  —We can help the church sustain and innovate for greater influence.

- **Level Four (71-89):** *Striving for quality*

  —We can help the church advance to the next step.

- **Level Three (51-70):** *Secure and faithful*

  —We can help the church take the next step towards full commitment.

- **Level Two (31-50):** *Scratching the surface*

  —We can help the church overcome its challenges and move forward.

- **Level One (20-30):** *Struggling to move forward*

  —We can help the church organize and strengthen its efforts.

At Bridge Ministries, Inc. (BMI), our PrayerMatters services are designed to help churches and individuals improve and/or sustain their prayer lives. We can help your church get to the next level and beyond. Visit us at *www.BrigdeMinistriesInc.com* to learn more about our 40 Days of Prayer Initiative (40-DPI), to schedule your free 30-minute discovery session with our Founder, Dr. Hugh Wesley Carrington, or to book him to launch your 40-DPI.

PART I SCORING GRID				
Section One	**Strongly Agree**	**Agree**	**Disagree**	**Strongly Disagree**
Prayer is the fundamental biblical principle that should guide a church's activities (its ministries and programs).	2.5	2	1	0.5
The church's prayer life (its commitment to prayer) can positively impact the surrounding community.	2.5	2	1	0.5
The level of spiritual growth in a church can be strengthened through corporate prayer.	2.5	2	1	0.5
Prayerless Christians (church members) can impede the proper functioning of a church.	2.5	2	1	0.5
A prayer strategy should lead the spiritual, membership, and financial growth strategy for a church.	2.5	2	1	0.5

Section Two	**Yes**	**No**
Is there a spiritual environment in your church that supports prayer and prayer related activities?	2.5	0.5
Does your church have a prayer champion(s), i.e., someone with a profound understanding of the importance of prayer in God's house (your church) and supports it?	2.5	0.5
Does your church view individuals, practices, and/or things that are hindering its spiritual growth and development as a threat?	2.5	0.5
Is your church recognized by the community as a place of prayer?	2.5	0.5
Is the attendance at prayer meeting worship service significantly lower, when compared with other worship services?	0.5	2.5

Section Three	Strongly Disagree	Disagree	Agree	Strongly Agree
Cultivating and maintaining an organizational culture and worship structure where consistent corporate and personal prayer is the norm, is practiced at my church.	0.5	1	2	2.5
In my church, prayer plays a prominent role in the lives of members and chiefly in the lives of church leaders.	0.5	1	2	2.5
My church is not simply going through the motions, and focuses on genuine prayer and worship, week after week.	0.5	1	2	2.5
My church does not need to change its assumptions, ways of thinking about, and approach to prayer.	0.5	1	2	2.5
My church's primary function, first and foremost, is to be a house of prayer.	0.5	1	2	2.5

Section Four	Yes	No
Is prayer worship?	2.5	0.5
If your church were to schedule a prayer meeting service and a game night, would the attendance at game night be better?	0.5	2.5
Is prayer included in the mission and vision statements of your church?	2.5	0.5
Are the church's ministries adding spiritual value to the community?	2.5	0.5
Does your church spend quality time in prayer at committee and planning meetings?	2.5	0.5

PART II SCORING GRID				
Section Five	**Strongly Disagree**	**Disagree**	**Agree**	**Strongly Agree**
I think prayer, as a central worship practice, has been removed from the center of my church.	2.5	2	1	0.5
The legacy of prayerlessness in my church is negatively impacting our surrounding community.	2.5	2	1	0.5
I've witnessed that there is a correlation between my church's spiritual weakness and its lack of corporate prayer.	2.5	2	1	0.5
Prayerless Christians (church members) are impeding the proper functioning of my church.	2.5	2	1	0.5
A prayer strategy is not leading the spiritual, membership, and financial growth strategy for my church.	2.5	2	1	0.5

Section Six	**Yes**	**No**
Is the level of unity (oneness, one accord) great among members at your church?	2.5	0.5
In your church, is more time allocated for Bible study, singing and/or preaching, when compared to time spent praying?	0.5	2.5
In your church, are the youth and children excited about prayer?	2.5	0.5
Do all of the worship services in your church reflect prayer as a priority?	2.5	0.5
Are there individuals, practices, and/or things in your church preventing it from moving forward spiritually?	0.5	2.5

Section Seven	Strongly Agree	Agree	Disagree	Strongly Disagree
Churches should cultivate and maintain an organizational culture and worship structure where consistent corporate and personal prayer is the norm.	2.5	2	1	0.5
Prayer must play a prominent role in the lives of church members and chiefly in the lives of church leaders.	2.5	2	1	0.5
Churches should avoid the pitfall of simply going through the motions, week after week, when it comes to genuine prayer and worship.	2.5	2	1	0.5
Churches that are serious about prayer, usually change their assumptions, ways of thinking about, and approach to prayer.	2.5	2	1	0.5
The church's primary function, first and foremost, is to be a house of prayer.	2.5	2	1	0.5

Section Eight	Yes	No
During the last 3 months, have you preached or heard your pastor preach a sermon on prayer?	2.5	0.5
Does your church have a weekly prayer worship service where prayer, and only prayer, is the focus?	2.5	0.5
Are your members and visitors excited about prayer?	2.5	0.5
Does your church have and use prayer request cards and/or a prayer box?	2.5	0.5
Does your church have a vision for prayer (i. e. a clear awareness of what can and will happen when you and other members pray)?	2.5	0.5

A Guide to Reading and Praying
Through *Inevitable & Imminent* in 40 Days

And said unto them, It is written,
My house shall be called the house of prayer;
but ye have made it a den of thieves.

—MATTHEW 21:13 (KJV)

We have a fixed quantity of time that's on the verge of running out.

I don't know when, but I know that time is and will run out soon.

DAY 1

Read Pages: iii-ix (Preface)
Pray for spiritual discernment.

REFLECTIONS

_____

_____

_____

_____

_____

_____

DAY 2

Read Pages: xi-xvi (Three Presuppositions)
Pray about partnering with God to assist in finishing His work.

REFLECTIONS

_____

_____

_____

_____

_____

DAY 3

Read Pages: xvi-xxi (Inevitable and Imminent…)
Pray that this book disrupts your current way of thinking about prayer.

REFLECTIONS

_____

_____

_____

_____

_____

_____

DAY 4

Read Pages: 1-6
Pray for the capacity to embody and strength to cast the vision.

REFLECTIONS

_____

_____

_____

_____

_____

DAY 5

Read Pages: 6-10
Pray for the capacity to embody and strength to cast the vision.

REFLECTIONS

DAY 6

Read Pages: 10-17
Pray for the capacity to embody and strength to cast the vision.

REFLECTIONS

DAY 7

Read Pages: 19-21
Pray for the removal of spiritual robbers from your life and church.

REFLECTIONS

_____

_____

_____

_____

_____

_____

DAY 8

Read Pages: 22-25
Pray for the removal of spiritual robbers from your life and church.

REFLECTIONS

_____

_____

_____

_____

_____

_____

DAY 9

Read Pages: 25-33
Pray for the removal of spiritual robbers from your life and church.

REFLECTIONS

_____

_____

_____

_____

_____

_____

DAY 10

Read Pages: 35-37
Pray that you and your spiritual leaders proclaim your church to be a house of prayer.

REFLECTIONS

_____

_____

_____

_____

_____

DAY 11

Read Pages: 38-42
Pray that you and your spiritual leaders proclaim your church to be a house of prayer.

REFLECTIONS

_____

_____

_____

_____

_____

_____

DAY 12

Read Pages: 43-49
Pray that you and your spiritual leaders proclaim your church to be a house of prayer.

REFLECTIONS

_____

_____

_____

_____

_____

_____

DAY 13

Read Pages: 51-57
Pray that your church will develop and implement fruitful ministries.

REFLECTIONS

_____

_____

_____

_____

_____

_____

DAY 14

Read Pages: 57-61
Pray that your church will develop and implement fruitful ministries.

REFLECTIONS

_____

_____

_____

_____

_____

_____

DAY 15

Read Pages: 61-67
Pray that your church will develop and implement fruitful ministries.

REFLECTIONS

_____

_____

_____

_____

_____

DAY 16

Read Pages: 69-72
Pray that you will not be overcome by the attacks and distractions.

REFLECTIONS

_____

_____

_____

_____

_____

DAY 17

Read Pages: 72-77
Pray that you will not be overcome by the attacks and distractions.

REFLECTIONS

_____

_____

_____

_____

_____

_____

DAY 18

Read Pages: 79-81
Pray for the courage to walk away praying, if necessary.

REFLECTIONS

_____

_____

_____

_____

_____

DAY 19

Read Pages: 82-87
Pray for the courage to walk away praying, if necessary.

REFLECTIONS

_____

_____

_____

_____

_____

_____

DAY 20

Read Pages: 89-94
Pray for enough faith to try again.

REFLECTIONS

_____

_____

_____

_____

_____

_____

DAY 21

Read Pages: 94-101
Pray for enough faith to try again.

REFLECTIONS

_____

_____

_____

_____

_____

DAY 22

Read Pages: 103-105 (House of Prayer Process)
Pray for you and your church's spiritual maturity.

REFLECTIONS

_____

_____

_____

_____

_____

DAY 23

Read Pages: Reread, as needed, any portion of Chapter 1 to ensure understanding as you reflect on the question: have I embodied the vision?

Pray for the capacity to embody and strength to cast the vision.

A: The Vision
Have you embodied the vision?

REFLECTIONS

_____

_____

_____

_____

_____

_____

DAY 24

Read Pages: Reread, as needed, any portion of Chapter 2 to ensure understanding as you reflect on the question: Am I praying for the removal of spiritual robbers?
Pray for the removal of spiritual robbers from your life and church.

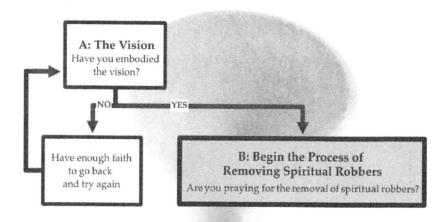

A: The Vision
Have you embodied the vision?

NO

YES

Have enough faith to go back and try again

B: Begin the Process of Removing Spiritual Robbers
Are you praying for the removal of spiritual robbers?

REFLECTIONS

DAY 25

Read Pages: Reread, as needed, any portion of Chapter 3 to ensure understanding as you reflect on the question: have I proclaimed my church to be a house of prayer?

Pray that you and your spiritual leaders proclaim your church to be a house of prayer.

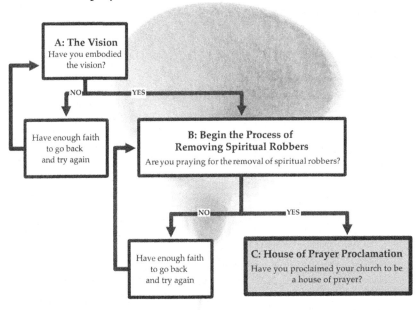

REFLECTIONS

_____

_____

_____

_____

_____

_____

DAY 26

Read Pages: Reread, as needed, any portion of Chapter 4 to ensure understanding as you reflect on the question: are we developing and implementing fruitful ministries?
Pray that your church will develop and implement fruitful ministries.

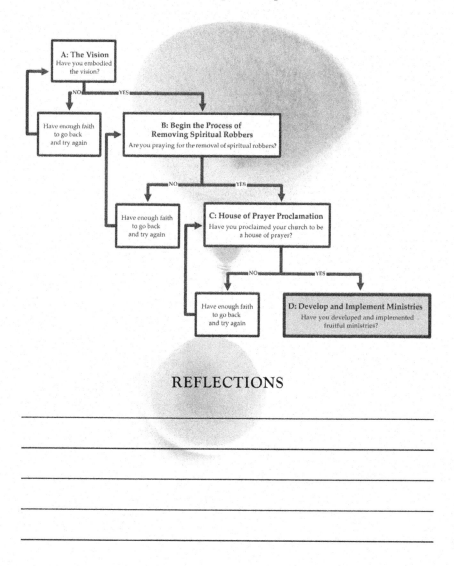

REFLECTIONS

_____

_____

_____

_____

_____

_____

DAY 27

Read Pages: Reread, as needed, any portion of Chapter 5 to ensure understanding as you reflect on the question: am I prepared for the attacks and distractions?

Pray that you will not be overcome by the attacks and distractions.

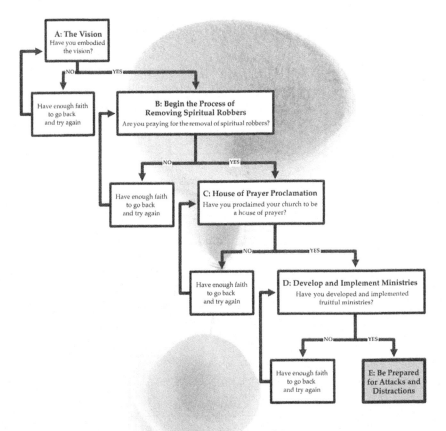

REFLECTIONS

_____

_____

_____

_____

DAY 28

Read Pages: Reread, as needed, any portion of Chapter 6 to ensure understanding as you reflect on the question: do I know when to walk away praying?

Pray for the courage to walk away praying, if necessary.

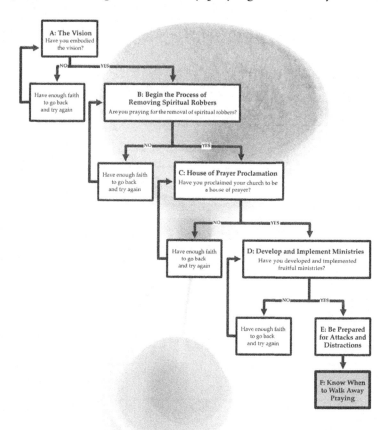

REFLECTIONS

_____

_____

_____

_____

DAY 29

Read Pages: Reread, as needed, any portion of Chapter 7 to ensure understanding as you reflect on the question: do I have enough faith to try one more time?

Pray for enough faith to try again.

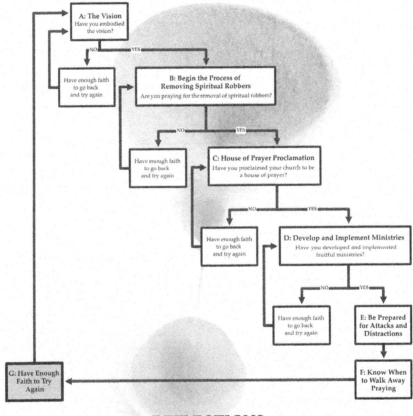

REFLECTIONS

_____

_____

_____

_____

DAY 30

Read Pages: 105-113 (House of Prayer Canvas)
Pray for clarity in developing the strategy for spiritual change and growth.

REFLECTIONS

_____

_____

_____

_____

_____

_____

DAY 31

Read Page: 108 (The Vision) Prayerfully consider each question and how you will challenge your church to become a house of prayer.
Pray for spiritual discernment.

REFLECTIONS

_____

_____

_____

_____

_____

DAY 32

Read Page: 108-109 (Spiritual Robbers and The Proclamation) Prayerfully consider each question and how you will challenge your church to become a house of prayer.
Pray for spiritual discernment.

REFLECTIONS

_____

_____

_____

_____

_____

_____

DAY 33

Read Page: 109 (Fruitful Ministries and Attacks and Distractions) Prayerfully consider each question and how you will challenge your church to become a house of prayer.
Pray for spiritual discernment.

REFLECTIONS

_____

_____

_____

_____

_____

DAY 34

Read Page: 109 (Walk Away Praying and Try Again) Prayerfully consider each question and how you will challenge your church to become a house of prayer.
Pray for spiritual discernment.

REFLECTIONS

_____

_____

_____

_____

_____

_____

DAY 35

Read Pages: 115-123
Pray that you never hear or experience the pronouncement.

REFLECTIONS

_____

_____

_____

_____

_____

DAY 36

Read Pages: 123-131
Pray that you never hear or experience the pronouncement.

REFLECTIONS

_____

_____

_____

_____

_____

_____

DAY 37

Read Pages: 133-138
Pray for the latter rain that will allow us to co-labor with God to finish His work.

REFLECTIONS

_____

_____

_____

_____

_____

_____

DAY 38

Read Pages: 138-145
Pray for the latter rain that will allow us to co-labor with God to finish His work.

REFLECTIONS

_____

_____

_____

_____

_____

DAY 39

Read Pages: 146-151
Pray for the latter rain that will allow us to co-labor with God to finish His work.

REFLECTIONS

_____

_____

_____

_____

_____

DAY 40

Read Pages: 151-159

Pray for the latter rain that will allow us to co-labor with God to finish His work.

REFLECTIONS

_____

_____

_____

_____

_____

_____

DAY 41... KEEP PRAYING!

We often set aside 40 days, 2 weeks, 7 days, a special day, or specific hours for prayer. In too many of our churches prayer is an initiative (a cyclic program) when it should be a constant—a perpetual church pursuit. I don't have a problem with setting aside time for prayer; I'm more concerned with the unintended consequences. When we exclusively approach prayer (our approach to the throne of God) in this manner, we send the wrong message to our congregations. While it is not our intent, we send the message that now is the time you should *really* be praying and for how long. These prayer initiatives set unintentional limits on how long we pray and the intensity of our prayers and create a bipolar spiritual experience in our churches.

I've witnessed the bipolar spiritual experience over and over again in many churches. Individuals and the collective church are on fire—a spiritual high—for 40 days or 2 weeks, and then they return to business as usual. We get to the end of the allotted time for prayer, and we stop praying. If it does not halt immediately, within a few weeks the amount and intensity of prayer wanes and stops. Over time we become conditioned to praying, stopping, and starting again. Now we're praying; now we're not. Accordingly, there is limited-to-no sustainability or continuity in such cycles of prayer for a church to develop and grow spiritually.

What a radical change and spiritual benefit to our individual members and to the collective church and community if we were able to engender the same level of faithful prayer and expectancy of answers throughout the year, every year! Would it not be wiser to encourage our churches to develop a habit of prayer every day of the year? Churches cannot afford to focus on prayer for 40 days, 2 weeks, 7 days, special days, or specific hours exclusively. Prayer should be a daily experience that is accentuated when the collective church gathers throughout the week for worship. Daily intense prayer (absent the temporary highs and lows—the bipolar spiritual experience) must be a constant in the life of a church and the individual Christian.

p. 123-124, 126

Notes to the Reader

Inevitable & Imminent: On Becoming a House of Prayer—The Process can also be used to teach a credit course at the college or university level or as a non-credit course sponsored by your local church. Dr. Carrington is available to teach this course and/or to work with instructors to buildout a syllabus for a semester (15 weeks) course, to include:

- Learning Outcomes
- Spiritual Context and Rationale
- Assignments and Grading
- Evaluation Process and Rubrics

Course Title: House of Prayer Essentials

Required Texts
- The Holy Bible
- *Inevitable & Imminent: On Becoming a House of Prayer— The Process*

Sample Weekly Schedule

Unit	Topic	Readings[1]	To Do
Week 1	Course Overview & Logistics Group Assignments…		
Week 2	The Case for Prayer	Preface & Introduction	House of Prayer Assessment Due
Week 3	The Vision	Chapter 1	
Week 4	Spiritual Robbers I	Chapter 2	Group Project Summary Due
Week 5	Spiritual Robbers II	Chapter 2	Reflection Paper #1
Week 6	The Proclamation	Chapter 3	Reflection Paper #2
Week 7	Fruitful Ministries I	Chapter 4	Reflection Paper #3
Week 8	Fruitful Ministries II	Chapter 4	Reflection Paper #4 Church Leader Interview Report Due
Week 9	Attacks and Distractions	Chapter 5	Reflection Paper #5
Week 10	Walk Away Praying	Chapter 6	Reflection Paper #6
Week 11	Try Again	Chapter 7	Reflection Paper #7
Week 12	The House of Prayer Process and Canvas	Chapter 8	Reflection Paper #8
Week 13	The Pronouncement I	Chapter 9	Reflection Paper #9
Week 14	The Pronouncement II	Chapter 9	
Week 15	End-Time Work	Conclusion	
Week 16	**Finals Week: House of Prayer Implementation Plans and Presentations Due**		

[1] Additional current readings, cases, videos, and/or activities will be assigned to enhance and support learning outcomes.

Visit us at *www.BridgeMinistriesInc.com* to hear the unedited sermon that was the basis for this book.

On our website, you can also learn more about our companies and the services that are designed and available for churches and religious organizations. At Bridge, Inc., we provide innovative solutions for more abundant living.

Our member companies include:

- **Bridge Ministries, Inc. (BMI)** — PrayerMatters
- **Bridge Consulting, Inc. (BCI)** — Organizational Learning & Development
- **Bridge Research, Inc. (BRI)** — Research & Evaluation
- **Bridge Press, Inc. (BPI)** — Book Concept Development and Publishing

Bridge Ministries Consulting, Inc.

...take my people higher

Struggling with planning your prayer meetings? Thinking there's no way you can study and discuss prayer for 52 weeks? Yes, you can! In this new book, Hugh will consider crucial concepts on prayer that can be used to guide your prayer meeting discussions throughout the year. Stay connected with us and be one of the first to know when this new book, *The Church@Prayer: 52 Weeks at the Throne of Grace*, is released.

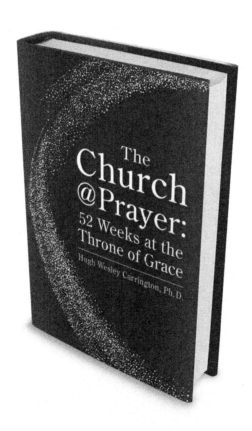

About the Auth

Hugh Wesley Carrington, Ph.D. is Lead Consul
Ministries Consulting, Inc. Hugh has held several a
positions in local churches of a denomination that numb
18 million worldwide. He is a frequent presenter at local
and related events and has had the opportunity to obser
we as Christians approach prayer. He has had the opportun.
implement what he teaches, including the house of prayer proc
and knows that it works.

Hugh is a process thinker and blends his love for education,
the study of people, and research as a consultant helping organizations optimize performance through staff training & development
and streamlining of organizational processes. In addition to being
the Lead Consultant at Bridge Ministries, Hugh is currently also
an Adjunct Professor at Long Island University in the School of
Business, the Department of Social Work, and the Department of
Sociology and Anthropology.

CPSIA information can be obtained
at www.ICGtesting.com
Printed in the USA
BVOW08s0922271017
498801BV00002B/2/P